PRAYING WITH PETER

Mary Jane Fischer

Praying With Peter
by Mary Jane Fischer
Copyright ©2007 Mary Jane Fischer

All rights reserved. This book is protected under the copyright laws of the United States of America. This book may not be copied or reprinted for commercial gain or profit.

Unless otherwise noted all Scriptures are taken from the New King James version of the Bible, Copyright ©1979, 1980, 1982 by Thomas Nelson, Inc. Used by permission.

Scripture quotations marked KJV are taken from the *Holy Bible, King James Version*. Verses marked TLB are taken from *The Living Bible*, Copyright ©1971 owned by assignment by Illinois Regional Bank N.A. (as trustee). Used by permission of Tyndale House Publishers, Inc., Wheaton, Illinois 60189. All rights reserved.

ISBN 978-1-58169-239-6
Library of Congress Control Number: 2007930476

For worldwide distribution.
Printed in the U.S.A.

Gazelle Press
P.O. Box 191540 • Mobile, AL 36619
800-367-8203

Table of Contents

INTRODUCTION VIII
PREFACE XI

CHAPTER ONE
Pilgrims 1
We Are Chosen 2
Blessing the Lord 4
Mercy 5
Inheritance 6
His Power 7
Trials 8
Genuine Faith 10
Joy 11
Remarkable Joy 12
Saving Grace 13
The Prophets 15
The Spirit of Christ 16
Growing Lessons 17
Our Mind 18
Old Habits 19
Call to Holiness 20
Understanding Holiness 21
Impartiality 22
Futile Traditions 23
Redeemed by the Blood 24
Revelation 25
Raised to Glory! 26
Fervent Love! 28
Life Eternal 29
Rest in Unrest 30
Eternal Word 31

CHAPTER TWO
Evil 32
Growing 33
Grace 34
Jesus! 35
A Spiritual House 36
Chief Cornerstone 37
We Who Believe 38

The Offending Rock	40
Special People	42
Mercy	43
Sojourners	44
Victory Over Evil	45
Submission	46
Doing Good	48
Use of Freedom	49
Honor People	50
Submission	51
Patience	52
The Call	53
Deceit	54
Commitment	55
Dead to Sin	57
Prodigals	58

CHAPTER THREE

Adaptations	59
Chastity	61
Influence	62
Gentleness, Quietness	63
Holy Women	64
Role of Women	65
Heirs Together	67
Compassion and Tenderness	68
Called to Bless	69
The Tongue!	70
Church Transgressions	72
Ears and Eyes	73
Doing Good	74
Threats	75
Our Responses	77
Clear Conscience	78
Suffer for Good	80
Dead Flesh	82
Called to Preach	84
Jesus' Longsuffering	85
Buried With Jesus	86
Our Great Intercessor	87

CHAPTER FOUR

Fellowship of Suffering	88
God's Will	89
Our Past	90
Remembering Our Past	91
Caregiving	92
Judging Others	93
God Equips	94
Watchful Prayer	95
Warm Love	96
Happy Hospitality	97
Gifts	98
Ministry	99
Understanding Trials	100
Enter Into Suffering	101
America's Freedom	102
Personal Behavior	104
Self-Will	105
Believers' Judgment	106
Saving the Righteous	107
Doing Good	108

CHAPTER FIVE

Motivators	109
Leading Others	111
Overworked Pastors	112
Leadership, Not Lordship	113
Be Crowned!	114
The Old Nature	115
The Spoiler	116
Humbling Ourselves	117
God Cares	118
Satan Is Real	119
The Armor	120
Brotherhood Sufferings	121
Experience the Glory!	122
Praise to the Lord!	123
Bonding	124
Accountability	125
Rich Tenderness	126

TOPICAL INDEX 127

Dedication

To my husband George,
I love you!

Acknowledgments

I owe much gratitude to my first mentor, Phyllis Shaw, whose patience and wisdom led me tenderly through the fascinating "first years" of rapid, spiritual growth.

To Jeanne Ahlfeld whose keen ears have always been my sounding board. Thank you for listening. To Jeanne Kendall, Karen Jones, and Jeanne Neely who read manuscript portions and gave valuable suggestions from a reader's viewpoint—thank you.

To my psychology professor, Gary Shaw, who has fielded questions and always given encouragement when most needed—I appreciate your loyal friendship.

To my agent, Keith Carroll, whose tactful remarks have caused me to dig deeper—thank you.

A big thank you to my sisters, Frances Anderson and Edith Caudle, who helped with the arduous task of proofreading. For the rest of my family who always stand by me in troublesome times—thank you for loving me!

Introduction

Praying With Peter for three reasons—

Love for my Lord.
Love for others.
A desire to see others grow into an exciting,
 productive relationship with the living Lord!

Churches across our land are teeming with those who haven't the foggiest idea of what it means to have a relationship with the living Christ. Perhaps they are under the same allusion I was under: "Do as the others do and surely I will make it to heaven someday."

The expression, a relationship with Jesus Christ is often espoused from pulpits but not explained effectively to listening ears. I heard it for years and thought I must have it. I was doing the things Christians do, such as,

Going to church regularly
Paying my tithe
Serving on committees
Helping with programs
Volunteering when volunteers were needed.
Enjoying the services and the warm community.

All of the above are good when one wants to support the church of their choice. None of the above will cause one to have a vital, growing relationship with the living Lord!

To discover the living Lord and have that vital relationship means we begin to interact with a living Presence in our lives—God with us! God is truly our Father, and He wants us to share our heart's desires and secrets with Him by talking to Him everyday.

Interacting with the living Lord means we are living in a close relationship—we walk with Him and He with us. We talk with Him and He with us! He leads us. His Holy

Spirit instructs us, and we become more and more aware of our responsibility to help build His earthly kingdom.

Jesus is our Friend. He came to earth as God Incarnate. He told us how to live and showed us with parables. He illustrated with hands-on lessons. He gave His innocent blood as a sacrifice for our personal sins. He promised He would send the Holy Spirit to be with us forever as our Comforter, Guide, and Leader into all truth.

I had understood the Trinity—Father, Son and Holy Spirit—for years; the three are one and cannot be separated. They are three but yet one. I accepted that. It wasn't until I was motivated enough to earnestly read the scriptures for myself on a daily basis that God's Holy Spirit, the third person of the Trinity, began to reveal truth. When this marvelous thing happened, it began to affect my heart!

It was a miracle. Truth became personalized: Jesus came to earth for me...Jesus died for me...He sent His Holy Spirit to lead and guide all Christians (including me) into all truth! I began to weep with joy each day as I read God's Word. I wept each time as I talked to the Lord. Tears of joy flooded my soul again and again. The Holy Spirit cleansed my soul often (and He still does). It was pure joy, hard to explain, but heavenly to experience.

Because I had become motivated enough to read God's Word for myself and bare my soul and share my life with God, my Father, on a daily basis, the Holy Spirit came to me. Indeed He touched me, and eventually I learned to allow Him to flow through me to help others.

I discovered truth each time I read God's Word and spent time thinking about it, talking to God about it, and rejoicing in this new relationship.

Now I knew what having a relationship with the living Lord meant and wanted to share the good news with the world in God's creative ways.

Praying With Peter is a result of spending time in

I Peter, verse-by-verse, and waiting upon the Holy Spirit to create words that form His prayers.

My prayer is that these exciting insights into the words of Peter will increase your love for the Lord and others, and give you an even greater desire to see all Christians grow into a productive relationship with the living Lord!

Preface

I selected First Peter as resource scriptures for this book of prayers because Peter reveals his innermost feelings so openly. He is emotional and not ashamed. He shares his faults and gives us, the readers, opportunity to relate. Through Peter I see my human nature as acceptable but also in need of more of God's mercy and grace.

Two important problems I have wrestled with in life are submission and suffering. Both are an inevitable part of life. Both are difficult lessons that I learn again and again. Peter effectively discusses these two problems. I believe all of us need to hear what the apostle has to say. I have benefited by taking his words to heart.

I wrestled with submission as a child who must obey parents. I wrestled with submission as a student who must adapt and submit to rules, regulations, and changing life challenges. How much unhappiness and discontent would be avoided if leaders and subordinates were submitted to one another in the best interests of all!

Many marriages could be improved and, yes, salvaged if couples understood the true concept of living a submissive life. Why? Because coupled with the concept of submission is respect for others, their opinions, ideas and thoughts. Our human nature is not one of natural submission, and Peter helps us see ourselves as we are.

The second major reason I chose the epistle of First Peter is that Peter understands the much misunderstood concept of suffering as it relates to growth in Christ. He opens a big window to allow the reader opportunity to accept suffering as a natural and inevitable part of life. More importantly, Peter shows us that suffering is the way we more affectively relate our lives to Christ. For example, do we meet our problems as believers or non-believers? Do we allow Christ to enter into our responses to pain and disappointment? Peter shows us with great clarity that when we accept suffering and walk through it with patience, God will open the doors wide enough for us to see and understand suffering as an opportunity and a blessing!

—

Mary Jane Fischer

"That He might sanctify and cleanse her [the Church] with the washing of water by the word."
(Eph. 5:26)

Chapter One
Pilgrims

Peter, an apostle of Jesus Christ, to the pilgrims of the Dispersion in Pontus, Galatia, Cappadocia, Asia, and Bithynia (I Peter 1:1)

Our Father and our God, how fortunate I am to be able to call myself a pilgrim! I have been chosen by You and set aside as one of Your special people, with a special call upon my life. I am on a journey with You. I am weak and will need Your help every day to make that journey.

Lord Jesus, I want to know You better, so help me open my heart to Peter, your impetuous follower, who revealed his humanness to everyone so openly. Help me become sensitive and vulnerable, just like Peter. As I open my heart to pray and study the words of First Peter, help me increase in passion, like Peter, and give me a fuller understanding of myself and how I relate to You.

Peter had a burning passion for You. Give me a burning passion too. Peter had a deep desire to fulfill the call upon his life. Help me deepen my commitment to fulfill Your call upon my life. I need a dedication similar to Peter's dedication in order to grow. Most of all, I need the willingness to tell You my feelings honestly as Peter did.

Help me understand this pilgrimage as a walk that will propel me forward through the deep valleys and plateaus as well as mountaintop experiences.

And now as I take a pilgrimage with Peter, let the words of the apostle speak to my heart in new ways. Help me realize the true meaning of being called a pilgrim. I am on a prayer journey with You. Help me yield myself to Your power and Your presence as You assist me with the leadership of Your precious Holy Spirit. In Jesus' name. Amen.

We Are Chosen

> ...elect according to the foreknowledge of God the Father, in sanctification of the Spirit, for obedience and sprinkling of the blood of Jesus Christ: Grace to you and peace be multiplied. (I Peter 1:2)

O Lord God, when I see the word "elect," it amazes me to think that You have chosen me as Your child because You say that You foreknew us all before the foundation of the world (Ro. 8:29). It is thrilling to know that not only are we all chosen, but also You have made provision for our sanctification by Your Holy Spirit.

Thank You for Your Spirit among us. Your Holy Spirit has wooed me from the beginning of my earthly existence. Long before I knew of Your love, Your precious Holy Spirit was calling to me. You didn't give up on me when I ignored Your call for many years. You ignored my selfish ways and loved me in spite of myself. What a miracle when I yielded and Your Holy Spirit touched me!

And since that day, how patient You have been with me in this process of sanctification. I have rebelled against Your gentle ways of teaching again and again. So often I have ignored Your gentle commands. Please forgive me.

But now what a joy to realize You will always come and gather me in again! Oh, keep me aware of Your Holy Spirit and Your gentle guidance. Help me obey Your voice. Your presence fills my day with assurance—the assurance that I am a work in process, and You will never leave me nor forsake me.

Peter tells us that it is the Holy Spirit who will help us increasingly understand better what Jesus did for us through His sacrifice of blood. Teach us again and again, Holy Spirit, about the blood of Jesus Christ shed for our sins. Let our hearts be so moved with gratitude that we grow to become strong disciples like Peter. With grateful hearts we receive Peter's blessing, "grace and peace be multiplied" in the holy name of Jesus. Amen.

"And let him who thirsts come.
Whoever desires, let him take of the water of life freely."
(Rev. 22:17b)

Blessing the Lord

Blessed be the God and Father of our Lord, Jesus Christ (1 Peter 1:3a)

How vividly I recall the first time I heard one of Your saints pray, "I bless You, O Lord." I could sense her deep love and devotion as she continued to worship You. As she prayed blessings upon You, Lord, the room filled with Your presence, and time stood still. I sat in awe and absorbed the sacredness of the moment.

Now I, too, feel worthy to bless You, O Lord. With all my heart and soul, my spirit blesses You; and my mind, will, and emotions desire to bless You. Thank You for the privilege of blessing others. Thank You for pouring Your love and grace through Your pilgrims when we seek more. What a privilege it is to say, "Bless you!" to others, and what a blessing we receive in return!

I bless You, O Lord. I think often of all Your benefits. Indeed, You forgive sin and often heal diseases. You execute justice for the oppressed. You make known to us Your ways and Your will through Your Word. You are merciful and slow to anger. You don't deal with us according to our sins, but You are gracious and continue to woo us tenderly to holiness by Your Spirit.

O Lord God, my heart bursts with gratitude when I think of Your bountiful goodness and the many reasons I have to express my love for You. Keep me in this attitude of praise, worship, and adoration as You lead me through another day. I pray in Jesus' name. Amen.

Chapter One

Mercy

...who according to His abundant mercy has begotten us again to a living hope through the resurrection of Jesus Christ from the dead. (1 Peter 1:3b)

Father, Your Word is so rich that I could dwell for days in just a few words. So often I praise You for Your mercy. I get lost in so many thoughts of Your unlimited goodness. The stress of living seems to melt slowly away when I'm meditating on Your Word. The abundance of Your mercy is unfathomable. I stop again and consider the power of the cross of Jesus Christ. What love! What compassion!

How do I begin to fully understand Your mercy? I was a sinner, but now I'm heaven bound. How glorious it will be to enter into the praise and worship of the many angels around Your throne, the living creatures and the elders in eternity who are crying out in gratitude, "Worthy is the Lamb who was slain to receive power and riches and wisdom, and strength and honor and glory and blessing!" (Rev. 5:12)

Thank You for Your mercy that endures forever. Because of Your mercy, I've been given a new birth and new life. O happy day when my spirit was aroused by the miraculous power of Your touch! Thank You for a new beginning. I praise You for a "living hope" given through the resurrection of Jesus Christ from the dead.

This living hope creates powerful excitement and gives energy to my days. This hope gives an abundance of joy that overflows in living witness. O Father, how do I show my gratitude for Your mercy? Help me to live in constant praise and worship. Help me release Your joy so that it might bless another person today. I pray all of these things in the strength and precious name of my Lord and Savior, Jesus Christ. Amen.

Inheritance

...to an inheritance incorruptible and undefiled and that does not fade away, reserved in heaven for you. (1 Peter 1:4)

My Father and my God, I contemplate this incorruptible inheritance reserved in heaven for all believers; it brings overwhelming gratitude from my heart. Feelings of fatigue and discouragement seem to flee away when I spend time with You. When I think of this heavenly treasure that is reserved for me, I feel only awe and words are inadequate.

Thank You that I will forever have all the wonders You have promised to all believers. I have abundant confidence in Your promises because of Your Spirit's seal upon me. Your seal guarantees that You will bring me to Yourself (Eph. 1:13-14).

It's amazing to think I have this gift waiting for me at the end of this life, and not only that, I am experiencing some of that inheritance even now. Thank You for the mark of Your Holy Spirit that You place upon my life. My spirit bears witness with Your Spirit, and I know this world cannot damage or corrupt this inheritance. It is reserved in heaven for true believers. Nothing can make it fade away. Hallelujah!

Thank You for this eternal kingdom that You have been preparing for believers from the foundation of the world. Thank You that Your grace is sovereign, my inheritance is free, and it is Your desire that everyone receive this gift.

Today, O Lord, help me tell of this glory and grace by sharing the gift of eternal life with others. I pray all of these things in the precious and holy name of Jesus Christ, who died for me. Amen.

Chapter One

His Power

...who are kept by the power of God through faith for salvation ready to be revealed in the last time.
(1 Peter 1:5)

Father, I think often of Your power in the earth. Your power is portrayed in all of life—the skies, the seas, the wonder of every little creature. You've created all for our pleasure. Who can deny the wonder of Your hand? The clock keeps ticking, the earth keeps revolving, the sun rises and the sun sets, and Your faithfulness endures forever!

The power of Your presence in my life causes my heart to quicken. I rejoice when I think of how I am kept by Your power through faith—nothing is impossible with You! Thank You that this incorruptible inheritance of eternal life is protected by Your power. The gift of faith assures me of that salvation.

I release faith this morning, as I praise You for the universe and all of its glory. I release faith as I look into the day You have created. I glory in the power of Your presence. You allow me to experience Your power through faith, and You will keep me through Your power unto eternal life or that exciting day when Jesus comes in all His glory.

You have touched me today through prayer. Now my faith looks up to You as I pray for others. Love, touch, heal, and provide for them as I name them one by one. Thank you for refreshing me. Help me to touch the lives of others. I pray these things in Jesus' powerful name. Amen.

Trials

> In this you greatly rejoice, though now for a little while, if need be you have been grieved by various trials... (1 Peter 1:6)

Thank You, Lord God, that rejoicing is Your instruction for Christians. I rejoice in Your mercy. I rejoice in living hope because of the sacrifice Jesus made for all of us. I rejoice in Jesus' resurrection from the dead. I rejoice in my promised inheritance that is incorruptible, undefiled, and does not fade away. I rejoice in the power of God that operates through the gift of faith. I rejoice in this daily walk of salvation—salvation that is in process right now, and will be revealed in all its glory when I meet You face to face.

Father, not only do I rejoice in these things, but I do rejoice in the hard times. Thank You for the valleys, the pain of unexpected sorrows, and the effects of evil that are committed against me and other Christians. All Christians have problems, just as unbelievers have problems. Thank You for grace to walk through the hard times.

The days have been hard, precious Jesus. I need the warmth of Your love this morning. Surround me. Put Your arms around me and hold me close as I weep soft tears of joy in Your presence. Thank you for touching me as I lean upon You with my pain. Thanking You is difficult when the going gets tough, but tough days seem to drive me farther along in my search for more of You.

Strengthen all who are going through heavy trials today. Give us patience, understanding, and a willingness to wait upon You and Your solutions. Forgive us for the times we complain. Remind us, "Your grace is sufficient for us, for Your strength is made perfect in weakness." Let us, like the apostle Paul, learn to "boast in our infirmities that the power of Christ rest upon us" (2 Cor. 12:9). We

Chapter One

boast in Your glory, Lord Jesus, and pray in Your name. Amen.

"That He might sanctify and cleanse her [the Church] with the washing of water by the word."
(Eph. 5:26)

Genuine Faith

> ...that the genuineness of your faith, being much more precious than gold that perishes, though it is tested by fire, may be found to praise, honor, and glory at the revelation of Jesus Christ... (1 Peter 1:7)

O Father, thank You for the richness of this life with its experiences that continue to teach me the hard lessons that You want me to learn. You give me strength when I am tired, and You encourage me when I am discouraged. You walk me through difficult days. You never let me down.

Thank You for the gift of faith and the freedom of will that You give me to help mold my faith. Thank You for trusting me with this powerful freedom of will. I am especially thankful for Your patience with me as I make daily decisions that affect the plan You have for my life.

Lately I have been tested physically, emotionally and spiritually. Often I have failed You. My responsibilities sometimes overwhelm me, and my words become harsh. Sometimes I indulge in self-pity, and sorrow causes me to feel depressed. Then I reach up. Thank You, Holy Spirit, for being my Counselor. Thank You for touching me when I turn to You for help. Thank You for bringing me to acknowledge my weaknesses. I swallow my pride and ask for forgiveness. Once again I experience the wonder of cleansing and restoration.

Enter into my decision-making today. I want to grow, precious Lord. I want to be an overcomer. Test me with fire so that my faith may be found to Your praise, honor, and glory. Help me stand up for You in all that I experience today. Help me to be found faithful until Jesus comes. I pray this in His precious name. Amen.

Chapter One

Joy

...whom having not seen you love. Though now you do not see Him, yet believing, you rejoice with joy inexpressible and full of glory... (I Peter 1:8)

Father, for years it seemed that faith was a mystery. I thought some people had it and others just couldn't believe. As a believer who had very little faith (and didn't know it), I remember asking another, "You mean that if you pray for something here, miles away something is going to happen because of your prayers?" She was astounded and said, "Why, yes!"

Now, some years later, because I have a relationship with Jesus, I believe! What made the difference? I became convinced through the lives and testimony of others that if Christianity was to ever become meaningful in my life, reading Your Word and talking to You on a regular basis was necessary.

Thank you, Father, that my faith grows as I read the Bible. My faith is deepening when I pray. Talking to You is natural and exciting. Sharing your love with others is becoming more and more spontaneous. The unearned blessing is that after I talk to You, Lord, there is deep joy and rejoicing that carries me throughout the day. Thank You for this inexpressible joy that is full of Your glory. In Jesus' name I pray. Amen.

Remarkable Joy

...whom having not seen you love. Though now you do not see Him, yet believing, you rejoice with joy inexpressible and full of glory. (1 Peter 1:8, repeated verse)

Thank You for Your Word that brings life to my spirit and joy to my soul. Because of You, Jesus, I'm aware of an inner joy that bubbles up like a fountain. This abiding joy affects all of life when I begin my days with You. Forgive me for those times I'm careless and do not take time for You.

I do love You, Lord Jesus, even though I've never seen You. I believe the Word and receive it daily into my heart. Thank You for the confidence it builds. I am awed at the scriptures that confirm and strengthen my faith, "...whom having not seen You love. Though now You do not see Him, yet believing, You rejoice with joy inexpressible and full of glory."

You create joy daily in my heart and continue to recreate me as I express gratitude to You day after day. This is a miracle and difficult to explain. Only You, by Your Spirit, can supply words to explain this indescribable, inexpressible joy. Hallelujah Jesus! Thank You, precious Savior! I rejoice in Your name. Amen.

Chapter One

Saving Grace

...receiving the end of your faith—the salvation of your souls. (1 Peter 1:9)

Father, as a young girl, I was taught that those who wanted eternal life should receive Jesus Christ. Jesus would come into their hearts and become Lord of their surrendered lives. I understood that this event was called "receiving the gift of salvation."

As I have grown into adulthood, I realize that salvation is much more than a one-time event. Salvation is a gift to be activated when believers seek more of You. How exciting it has been since I realized salvation is a process that began when I acknowledged Jesus Christ as my Lord and Savior!

Thank You for that day when I began to earnestly seek more of You. I turned from my old way of life, repented of my sins, and received You as my Lord and Savior. Truly, old things were passed away, and all things became new and exciting. Now I understand that salvation means that You delivered me from my former sins, and You are delivering me now as I daily submit to Your guidance and Lordship. Lord, what a glorious day of final deliverance it will be when my faith is consummated in Your heavenly presence!

That's why, precious Jesus, I walk out my salvation with fear and trembling. It was given to me as a free gift when I turned from my way of life to Yours. My salvation is nurtured as I yield to Your Lordship through prayer, and it will be completed when I'm able to say I have fought— and completed—the good fight. Yes, when I'm able to say, "I've finished the race, and joyfully kept and nurtured the gift of faith" (see 2 Timothy 4:7).

In the meantime, what an awesome experience is this walk with You! Thank You, Holy Spirit, for Your leadership and the power You give to overcome the daily temptations of life. I praise You from the bottom of my heart that I'm able to look forward to receiving the end of my faith, the completion of the salvation of my soul when Jesus comes. Hallelujah! I pray joyfully in the precious name of Jesus. Amen.

"And let him who thirsts come.
Whoever desires, let him take of the water of life freely."
(Rev. 22:17b)

Chapter One

The Prophets

Of this salvation the prophets have inquired and searched carefully, who prophesied of the grace that would come to you... (1 Peter 1:10)

Father, it seems that the days on this earth are fraught with greater and greater stress. It is difficult to find that precious time to spend with You. When I set aside time to read and pray, there seem to be priorities that constantly consume my mind and heart. Forgive me, Lord, and help me overcome the temptation to begin other tasks before allowing You to refresh my mind, heart, and soul with Yourself.

I need Your help today in everything that needs to be done. So I lay down my lists, my pressing chores, my desire to get things done, and my fear of the clock which ticks away precious minutes, and come to You in my weakness. Help me with the guidance and strength only You can give for the day.

Your Word tells me that the prophets of old relied upon the Spirit of God within them to inspire and instruct them in all they needed to know. So we, in these stressful times, need Your touch every day. Thank You for revealing Yourself through the prophets. They spoke of Your grace then, and their words continue to speak and inspire us today. Fill us with Your grace that we might reflect You today. In Jesus' name. Amen.

The Spirit of Christ

...searching what, or what manner of time, the Spirit of Christ who was in them was indicating when He testified beforehand the sufferings of Christ and the glories that would follow. (1 Peter 1:11)

O Father, how clearly this verse reveals to me the mysterious way Your Holy Spirit worked in the hearts of humans in the Old Testament. The prophets were aware that God was speaking through them when often they did not understand the words that the Holy Spirit was commanding them to say.

Thank You for their obedient, searching hearts. Thank You for the lessons I can learn from those who shared these truths that impart hope to God's children. I especially thank You for showing me that I am to walk in that kind of faith today—not always understanding Your direction but trusting Your wisdom above my human reasoning.

Will the body of Christ ever fully understand why You sent Christ to suffer for us and die on the cross for our sins? We cannot ever fully understand. Thank You for Your love that has no limit as to its width and length and depth and height.

How can our finite minds ever understand the riches of Your glory that have come to us who believe? We never shall, but oh, the joy of seeking more and more of You! Thank You, Lord, for Your presence and for glorious expectations that are filling us now. Help us let Your light shine through us today. In Jesus' name. Amen.

Chapter One

Growing Lessons

To them it was revealed that, not to themselves, but to us they were ministering the things which now have been reported to you through those who have preached the gospel to you by the Holy Spirit sent from heaven—things which angels desire to look into. (1 Peter 1:12)

Father, when I think of the prophets of the Old Testament, I wonder how they must have felt. They surely knew that You were speaking through them, but they couldn't possibly understand when and for whom their prophecies would be fulfilled. Thank You for their obedience to Your voice.

Help me grow from these powerful lessons given us by the prophets. They walked in obedience daily as they spoke of the grace and truth that would come to us through Jesus Christ—a grace and truth they yearned for themselves.

How blessed we are today in comparison to the prophets in the Old Testament! Now we know and more fully understand (as much as our finite minds will allow) who Jesus is, why He came, why He suffered, and why we are privileged to experience the glory of His presence while serving Him. Thank You for Your Word and for those who preach the Gospel in the power of the Holy Spirit sent from heaven. In Jesus' name. Amen.

Our Mind

Therefore gird up the loins of your mind, be sober, and rest your hope fully upon the grace that is to be brought to you at the revelation of Jesus Christ... (1 Peter 1:13)

Father, I thank You again and again for the gentleness of Your Holy Spirit. He is so gentle and yet firm as He admonishes me from time to time. Thank You for the command that I gird up the loins of my mind, be sober, and rest my hope fully upon the grace that is revealed to me through knowing Jesus Christ.

When I think of the wonder of all You've created, I am overwhelmed. When I think of my mind, its possibilities, and the way You've ordered it to function, I am amazed. When I consider mankind (all of us) as the capstone of Your creation, I marvel at the confidence and trust You have put in man. What a role You've given us in building Your kingdom on earth!

And You, Lord God, are admonishing me to order my mind. You are telling me to use my mind to its fullest to fulfill Your plans; You expect me to do this to help build Your earthly kingdom. Thank You for a mind so intricate, so delicate, and yet so powerful.

We have such a great capacity to think, reason, and understand, yet I am told the amazing mind is seldom used to its fullest capacity. Forgive us for sometimes being mentally lazy. Help us become daily learners. Give us a burning desire to seek You daily. Help us to become seekers. Help us use our minds more fully for the purpose of building Your kingdom on earth. In Jesus' name. Amen.

Chapter One
Old Habits

> *...as obedient children, not conforming yourselves to the former lusts, as in your ignorance... (1 Peter 1:14)*

Today's schedule is full of obligations, so many needs for prayer, and so many sick and hurting people. Thank You for the Rock that is higher, the shelter that's always available, and the Counselor who knows about these needs before I ask. Thank You for Jesus, my Friend, with whom I can talk every day, all day, and all night long.

Father, I come praising You for the stability that comes only from You. The world seems to be getting shakier and crazier all the time, but You keep me strong in the midst of chaos. Truly You are a steadying influence for all of us—the Rock of our refuge. Thank You that You never leave nor forsake us.

Thank You for calling us "Your obedient children" and challenging all of us to walk in newness of life. Increase our faith, Lord God, that we may willingly desire to obey You. As I think about Your Word today, I'm so glad that the freedom I find in You continues to increase as I obey the gentle voice of Your Holy Spirit.

You remind me that former habits can still weigh me down if I allow them to control me. This happens on occasion, but I thank You that I have moved from ignorance into the light of Your love. Help me where I am the weakest so that the things of this world (temptations) will grow strangely dim in the light of Your glory and grace. Thank You for the glorious light that calls us to greater obedience. Thank You for hearing my praises. I love You, precious Jesus, and pray these things in Your name. Amen.

Call to Holiness

...but as He who called you is holy, you also be holy in all your conduct, because it is written, "Be holy, for I am holy." (1 Peter 1:15-16)

Father, I've been spending time with Your command that we live holy lives. I tremble at Your words, "But as he which hath called You is holy, so be ye holy in all manner of conversation; Because it is written, 'Be ye holy; for I am holy'" (1 Peter 1:15-16 KJV). I am able to think of conducting myself in good ways, but it is so demanding to think of being holy in all manner of conversation. I need to be reminded again and again of James 1:26: "If anyone among you thinks he is religious and does not bridle his tongue but deceives his own heart, this one's religion is useless."

Oh, the power of the tongue! I might look out the back window and say, "The sun is shining so gloriously, it's going to be a day full of excitement!" Or I might say, "Oh dear, look at that bright sun. It's going to heat things up like an oven today." Lord, I realize that the power of my tongue creates an atmosphere in my home. My tongue governs the tone of conversations I have with others. My tongue affects my telephone calls; my interactions with family, work, business associates; and everything else I do. Help me always to control my tongue.

Holiness commands a hopeful, cheerful response, even in the midst of hectic living. So help me look at experiences and people today through Your eyes and react in positive ways. I need Your help, Lord. Move me away from old habits and old conduct. Forgive me for my weaknesses and fill me with Your power that will help me overcome these weaknesses. Lead me forward in the holy life You desire for every believer. I pray in Jesus' name. Amen.

Chapter One

Understanding Holiness

...because it is written, "Be holy, for I am holy."
(1 Peter 1:16, repeated verse)

O Father, who among us can contemplate Your holiness and fully comprehend it? I cannot! You are an awesome God, and I praise You. You meet all my needs, and I am so thankful for Your generous blessings. You command the operation of our universe. I know Your hand is always in control. But it is impossible for me to explain Your holiness.

You call us to holiness because You want us to emulate our Lord and Savior, Jesus Christ. Nothing is impossible with You, dear Lord, so I know You will help me in my weaknesses. I call for Your assistance. Just as You are patient with us, I believe You want us to be patient with others and ourselves. We cannot make ourselves holy—only You, by Your Holy Spirit, are able to direct us forward toward Your command, "Be holy, for I am holy."

I like Your promise that tells me "to increase in love and abound in love" and if I do this, "You will establish my heart blameless in holiness" (see 1 Thess. 3:12). Thank You for this challenge. Give me the patience to understand that this established heart, blameless in holiness, will only come to pass totally when the Lord Jesus Christ comes with all His saints.

Lord God, this gives me a longer, extended picture of the holiness to which You are calling us. It gives me hope and encouragement to walk out each day in Your love, while praying that I will abound in this glorious love toward others. Come, Holy Spirit, cleanse me and fill me with the boundless love of Jesus, so that I might touch and help others today. I look forward to someday having my heart established, blameless in holiness. In Jesus' name. Amen.

Impartiality

> And if you call on the Father, who without partiality judges according to each one's work, conduct yourselves throughout the time of your stay here in fear... (1 Peter 1:17)

Father, I thank You that the apostle Peter expected believers to call upon You often as they journey through this life. What would life be without communication with You?

But sometimes I find myself getting discouraged, and my life's goals and plans becoming uncertain. Then I realize it's because I haven't been spending time with You in prayer and praise. Thank You for this repeated lesson that I need Your presence in my life every day. The words of an old hymn run through my mind: "I Need Thee Every Hour!" Another hymn tells me that, through prayer, my heart unfolds like a flower before You; and as I acknowledge that every hour, You become as all brightness in my life.

Not only does calling upon You open my heart before You, but it also seems to melt any clouds of sin or sadness. Darkness and doubt are taken away. Some days I get too preoccupied and do not pray. Lord, forgive me. Deal with me according to my works. Teach me again that to walk in Your awesome presence, hour by hour and day by day, prayer is necessary.

You remind me that my petitions, as well as my temptations, are considered more fairly than I can ever imagine, according to Your divine plan for my life. Cause me not to question Your impartial judgments, Your afflictions, or Your other dealings with me—but cause me to trust Your fathomless wisdom as You weave Your pattern for my life. In Jesus' name. Amen.

Chapter One

Futile Traditions

...knowing that you were not redeemed with corruptible things, like silver or gold, from your aimless conduct received by tradition from your fathers. (1 Peter 1:18)

I feel tense this morning, Lord Jesus, so I come eagerly seeking Your help. I know that time spent with You will bring a quietness to my heart. Not only does Your presence bring quietness, but You quicken a song to my heart. It's an eternal song—a joy that doesn't cease, whether I'm sleeping or awake, whether I'm working or resting, whether I'm witnessing or studying. It's new life that You've instilled within me. I praise You for it!

Thank You that I'm redeemed, claimed for Christ, and written in the Lamb's Book of Life! Indeed, I wasn't redeemed with corruptible things like silver or gold, but I've been redeemed by the precious blood of Jesus.

Thank You, Father, that Jesus paid the ultimate price to free me from slavery. He freed me from the slavery of valuing earthly things. Now I value eternal things that make this life meaningful—peace, hope, joy, courage, and unselfishness. Thank You for the ransom paid for my freedom. Because of Jesus' love I am freed from the old life—the old, futile way of living—filled with giving too much credence to social status, beautiful homes, cars, clothes, and recognition.

Thank You for Jesus who satisfies my every longing. Thank You for His redeeming power that continues to rescue all who will seek Him. Keep us faithful to share with the unsaved as we recall our aimless conduct before redemption. I pray in His precious name. Amen.

Redeemed by the Blood

> ...but with the precious blood of Christ, as of a lamb without blemish and without spot. (I Peter 1:19)

Father, how I look forward to this quiet time! Thank You for the assurance that You await me with open arms as I do so need this time of restoration and cleansing. The days are often fraught with anxiety and stress. I need Your help to walk gracefully through the day. Thank You for the strength You give for daily living.

Lord God, daily I'm appreciating more deeply the precious blood of Christ, shed to take away my sins and the sins of the world. Thank You for bonding me with Yourself through the innocent shed blood of my Lord and Savior. O Father, I do not deserve this redemption, nor could I ever earn this redemption, but You so loved the world that You sent Your only Son to die for all. The blood of this precious Lamb who had no blemish or spot paid the price of our sin in lieu of our blood.

Thank You for our Savior who died so willingly that all who would receive Him as Lord and Savior could be forever bonded with You. Thank You for the Holy Spirit that Jesus sent to us when He went to be with You, Holy Father. It is the Holy Spirit who meets us in power and new life as we spend time with You in Your precious Word. Touch me again, Holy Spirit, with the truth of Jesus' supreme sacrifice! Cause my gratitude to continually deepen. In the name of the precious Lamb of Calvary who is worthy to be praised, I pray. Amen.

Chapter One

Revelation

He indeed was foreordained before the foundation of the world, but was manifest in these last times for you... (1 Peter 1:20)

Lord God, how I rejoice when I read the words in the Gospel of John that Jesus was the Word and that He was in the beginning with God. All things were made through Jesus, and nothing was made without Him (see John 1:1-3). Thank You that Jesus was foreordained before the foundation of the world and continues to manifest Himself to us through His Holy Spirit.

Thank You that Jesus sits at Your right hand, making intercession for us day and night. How comforting to know that we have an Intercessor who never stops praying for us. Father, help me follow the example of Jesus and try to become more like Him. Help me understand what it means to become a true intercessor for others.

Lord God, as Jesus continues to manifest Himself to the Church that was created by Him, I pray for the Church that it will become more sensitive to the manifestations of our Lord and Savior, Jesus Christ. Give us the courage to follow Your leading and forgive us when we quench Your Spirit.

Give us courage to accept the freedom You offer that we might praise You without restraint; in this freedom, we trust You will manifest Your presence more and more. Then, precious Lord, You enable us to go out equipped to share Your love in power. In Jesus' name. Amen.

Raised to Glory!

...who through Him believe in God who raised Him from the dead and gave Him glory, so that your faith and hope are in God. (1 Peter 1:21)

I rejoice in You, heavenly Father! Thank You for this joy that seems so constant. This joy is like a fountain that bubbles within because Your Spirit resides in my heart. Thank You for taking up residence within me. Help me nurture this new life daily with Your Word and prayer.

Father, Your Word tells me I believe in God because of Jesus. Thank You for our Savior who left the glory He had with You to come to earth. He humbled Himself as a man and taught us how to live in His three short years of ministry. What glory we experience now as Jesus' Holy Spirit leads us. Thank You for this Counselor who breathes eternal instruction to the human race.

I continue to ponder Your glory, O God, but realize I shall never fully understand or mentally define it to my satisfaction. You show us the glory of God in so many ways. You tell us we believe because You raised Jesus from the dead and gave Him glory so our faith and hope in You would be increased.

Thank You that Jesus completed all You sent Him to earth to do when He said, "It is finished." His obedience reminds us of His lofty goal for believers—that we are to become like Him. Thank You for raising Christ from the dead. His resurrection is Your glorious proclamation to the world that all power in heaven and earth was given to Jesus. He returned to heaven and was fully glorified with that same glory He possessed with You before He created the world.

This is more than my mind is able to comprehend, but I thank You that faith helps me understand it with my

Chapter One

heart. I praise You, Father, Son, and Holy Spirit. In Jesus' name. Amen.

"That He might sanctify and cleanse her [the Church] with the washing of water by the word."
(Eph. 5:26)

Fervent Love!

> Since You have purified your souls in obeying the truth through the Spirit in sincere love of the brethren, love one another fervently with a pure heart... (1 Peter 1:22)

Lord Jesus, how full and how rich Your Word seems as I tarry long to fully hear what You are saying to me! I am not always able to explain Your restorative, powerful influence during this time set aside for You, but I'm able to say, with great conviction, that time spent with You—reading, praying, and waiting—gives me fuel of love and grace for the day. It is difficult to explain, but beautiful to experience.

You remind me of Your words in Romans where You tell me as a born-again believer that I will allow Your love to be "poured out" to others. (See Ro. 5:5.) Now You are telling me that obeying Your truth will purify my soul. Thank You for telling me that it is Your Spirit who produces sincere love through me. Thank You for reminding me that this sincere love, which was given to me, is to be given away to others.

It sounds so simple. I am to spend time in Your Word, and the Spirit will reveal those things I need to see, understand, hear, and do. Yet I often weaken in my resolve and do not live in this obedience. Forgive me for my many weaknesses. Forgive me for the sin of busyness. I allow activities to crowd You out and fail to give You preeminence.

Fill me with this fervent love that has no limitations—this love that flows out from believers like a river when they abide in You! Purify my soul as I obey Your truth, through the Spirit, in sincere love of others. In Jesus' name. Amen.

Chapter One

Life Eternal

...having been born again, not of corruptible seed but incorruptible, through the word of God which lives and abides forever... (1 Peter 1:23)

Thank You, Father, that in the midst of busy days You remind me that if I seek You, I will find You. You say that Your kingdom is always to be sought first, and then all things will be added to my life (see Mt. 6:33).

I seek You today, dear Lord, in the midst of teeming responsibilities, decisions which weigh heavily upon me, and the guilt of not having the time to do for others the many things that would bring comfort and encouragement to their lives.

Help me, Father, to keep a healthy balance between what You expect of me and the many needs I see all around me. Thank You for the still, small voice of Your Holy Spirit who brings me comfort when I'm feeling guilty about my inability to stretch toward meeting the needs of others. Come this day, Holy Spirit, and bring the assurance that God will not require more from me than I'm able to handle.

Thank You, Holy Spirit, for Your power and presence in Your Word. You increase my joy in the knowledge that I have been born again, not of corruptible seed but incorruptible. You tell me that I have been born again through the Word of God that lives and abides forever. And thank You, Holy Spirit, for quickening my understanding.

Holy Father, as I have read Your Word today, it tells me that the work You've accomplished in my heart cannot be corrupted by any guilt heaped upon me since the work done in my heart will abide forever. In Jesus' name. Amen.

Rest in Unrest

...because all flesh is as grass, and all the glory of man as the flower of the grass. The grass withers, and its flower falls away... (1 Peter 1:24)

I seek You anxiously this morning, dear Father, as the world is chaotic. The days seem to be spinning with worldwide unrest. Thank You that in the midst of heavy responsibility and all this uncertainty, I have an anchor that will not let me go.

Teach me anew that this life I'm living is brief and is to be spent in preparation for a glorious eternal life with You. You tell me that all flesh is as grass, and grass lasts for only a little while and then is gone. And the same thing happens to all that I now take glory in—the work of my hands and my accomplishments on this earth will soon pass, just as the flowers of the grass will soon disappear.

So, Father, I look to the hope laid before me, the anchor of my soul, Jesus Christ, who is the only begotten of the Father, sent to shed His innocent blood that I might be forgiven and inherit eternal life.

Help me live this life in a world of unrest. Remind me again and again to lift my eyes unto the hills, for my help comes from You. Help me think of things above as more important than the accomplishments of this life, for too often my affections become fixed on earthly things.

Help me go forth as Your light that brings hope and peace where there may be anxiousness and unrest. Help my eyes look to You, my help in anxious times—the lifter of my burdens and the anchor of my soul. I pray in Jesus' name. Amen.

Chapter One
Eternal Word

*..."But the Word of the Lord endures forever."
Now this is the word which by the gospel was
preached to you. (1 Peter 1:25)*

O Holy Father, how I thank You for the light of this new day. The warmth of the sun streaming through the windowpane is only one reminder of the edifying warmth in this exciting time set aside to fellowship with You. Thank You for the assurance in my heart that Your Word is accompanied with Your presence. Fill me to overflowing during this quiet time of worship, expectancy, and awesome adoration. I wait upon You, Lord.

Thank You that the Word of the Lord endures forever. Thank You that Jesus is the Word and in Him all fullness dwells. When I think of the Word, which by the Gospel is preached, I'm reminded that we all may become Your preachers as we ask You to fill us daily with the power of the Gospel. Help us to be ministers today in our needy world. And dear Lord, along with our proclamations, let there be the powerful love of Jesus that reverberates with Your reconciliation, compassion, mercy, and understanding.

I pray, sweet Jesus, that my prayers may lead to definitive actions today. Activate my hands and feet in response to the motivation in my heart. I pray in Your name. Amen.

Chapter Two
Evil

Therefore, laying aside all malice, all deceit, hypocrisy, envy and all evil speaking... (1 Peter 2:1)

Father, I thank You for Your command that Christians lay aside all malice, deceit, hypocrisy, envy, and all evil speaking. Your Word keeps me in the path of life, and I have no choice but to obey Your commands (see I John 5:3). According to Your Word, Your commands are not difficult, but they seem very difficult at times. Please forgive me when I sin against You by surrendering to bad feelings and negative thoughts.

Thank You, Lord, that Your Word is quick, powerful, and sharper than any two-edged sword. It readily penetrates my heart. Your instruction commands that because we have accepted You as Lord of our lives, we should have no part of evil in any form. You leave no room for gossip or negative speaking in our lives as this is "evil speaking." I'm so thankful for Your Holy Spirit who polices my actions. Thank You, Holy Spirit, for bringing conviction to my heart when I fall into temptation. Thank You, Holy Father, for forgiving me when I grieve over my actions and ask for Your forgiveness.

Forgive me when I have stooped to express negative moods that have injured the body of Christ or added to another's sorrow with my negative attitude. Forgive me when I have failed to recognize those who need encouraging words. When I am discouraged myself, remind me that others are discouraged also. Fill my day with opportunities to reflect You, precious Lord, and give me sensitive eyes and ears. Have Your way with me. In Jesus' name. Amen.

Chapter Two

Growing

...as newborn babes, desire the pure milk of the word, that You may grow thereby... (I Peter 2:2)

*F*ather, Your Word is so plain. In order for us Christians to grow, we need the pure milk of the Word. All of us need to read the Bible, study it, and pray in response to the instruction You give us.

Your Word tells us that if we will seek You, we will find more of You. Father, I believe churches are full of infants who need the sincere milk of the Word. Help our leadership teach the body of Christ to seek You daily. Help our leadership teach that Your presence, Your power, and Your instruction become real when Christians read the Bible and talk to You often.

I recall the many years I spent as a Christian when I didn't understand the significance of reading Your Word daily for growth. Like many today, I believed that if I tried to be a good person, went to church on Sunday, gave to the church, and participated in church events, then I was surely doing what was required of me. I was putting forth effort to fulfill my role as a Christian.

Lord God, how grateful I am that, through the witness of others, You led me toward reading Your Word in earnest. In that earnestness, You baptized me in Your Holy Spirit, and "scales" were removed from my eyes. The miracle is that I've had an ongoing desire to seek You daily ever since.

Thank You for the wooing of Your Holy Spirit, the soft gentle call that again and again has caused me to turn from my way back to Your Word. I need the gentle cleansing and instruction given through Your Word and prayer to grow. Fill my cup, Lord, and make me a blessing to someone else today. In Jesus' name. Amen.

Grace

...if indeed you have tasted that the Lord is gracious. (1 Peter 2:3)

Father God, I experience your grace in the beautiful sunshine of this day. In the warmth of the sunshine I feel Your glorious, penetrating presence. Thank You for the gentle moving of the leaves as Your wind blows softly across the yard. These blessings remind me of Your grace, never ending and freely moving as You touch Your creation.

Touch us all today, Holy Spirit, that we might reflect Your love to our tense world. Let Your grace rest upon us and do a work in our hearts that reflects Your supernatural, irresistible love. Melt our hearts and humble us anew this morning. Come, Holy Spirit, and cleanse us so that more room will be made for God's manifold grace.

Thank You, Lord, that mere mortals have no corner on grace. Surely it is bigger than any idea our minds could ever grasp. Help us walk in this elusive gift as we attempt to follow in Your footsteps today. Without Your love and grace, we are nothing and have nothing to give to others. So bless us today with an abundance of Your magnificent grace. Indeed, we will have "tasted" that the Lord is gracious. In Jesus' name. Amen.

Chapter Two

Jesus!

Coming to Him as a living stone, rejected indeed by men, but chosen by God and precious...
(1 Peter 2:4)

Lord Jesus, thank You for drawing me close to You today. I come in full assurance of a warm welcome from You as God's chosen, elect and precious. Thank You for the expectation that fills my heart. I need this daily encounter with the "living stone," the Rock of my salvation.

As I contemplate the world into which I will step today, I ask that You fortify me to understand rejection as well as acceptance. Just as men rejected You, so those who have not tasted of Your grace will sometimes reject the message of those who represent You. Thank You that You commission every believer to represent You. It is an awesome but exciting responsibility. Give me the courage to witness boldly today.

What joy it must have been for the disciples to live with You and be taught by You! One wonders how You, precious Savior, could be rejected by the world—but You were. Thank You for the Word that portrays that rejection so vividly. Thank You for the Word that helps us understand rejection will come our way as we live for You in these days.

Today promises to be a busy day, Lord. Help me live it with Your grace. Lead me beyond myself that I might be a blessing to others. I pray in the name of Jesus, chosen by You and precious. Amen.

A Spiritual House

...you also, as living stones, are being built up a spiritual house, a holy priesthood, to offer up spiritual sacrifices acceptable to God through Jesus Christ. (1 Peter 2:5)

When I think of the words of that old hymn, "The Solid Rock," I rejoice in the foundation upon which I stand. So often when storms in life arise, I literally feel anchored upon my solid Rock, Jesus Christ. Thank You for this anchor that holds me steady in difficult times.

Each time a storm blows through my life, whether jealousy, criticism, circumstances, catastrophes, hardships, responsibilities, or things going wrong in general, my faith is tested. Thank You for testing my faith. It forces me to admit my weaknesses, and then I turn to You for help.

Thank You that You call Your children "living stones." You say we're a part of the spiritual house You are building on earth. Thank You for the body of Christ that's alive in You because of Jesus Christ. It is amazing to think that You are entrusting each of us to be one of Your "living stones." How awesome to be a part of that "holy priesthood" of earthly believers!

And Lord, You entrust us with this honorable responsibility so we will offer up spiritual sacrifices acceptable to You through Jesus Christ. The sacrifices that You want are yielded hearts, humbled in Your presence. I come humbly today, dear Lord, thanking You for the privilege of serving through Jesus Christ. Wash my hands today with the purity of Your Holy Spirit. In Jesus' name. Amen.

Chapter Two

Chief Cornerstone

Therefore it is also contained in the Scripture, "Behold, I lay in Zion a chief cornerstone, elect, precious, and he who believes on Him will by no means be put to shame." (1 Peter 2:6)

Father, the apostle Peter quoted from the prophet Isaiah when he called our beloved Savior a "chief cornerstone," elect and precious. Thank You for the promise that we who believe in Jesus Christ will not be put to shame. The Living Bible tells us, "We who believe in Jesus Christ will never be confused or disappointed!" (1 Peter 2:6 TLB)

Thank You, Lord God, for the gospel images given to us as believers that build our faith. We rest in the truth of this beautiful spiritual house that is being built of living stones on this earth right now. Strengthen all of us as living stones. How privileged we are to be an active part of this house!

Enliven me as one of Your stones today. Give me the willingness to be placed as a part of that which You are building. Cause me to yield to the part You want me to play today so that the body of Christ will continue to grow into a harmonious, living temple for Your glory.

Thank You for laying in the City of God that chief cornerstone, elect and precious, so that we who believe on Him will be guided with resolute confidence throughout this life. Most especially, I thank You for the opportunity to be one of Your living stones with Jesus Christ as the chief cornerstone. In Jesus' name. Amen.

We Who Believe

Therefore, to You who believe, He is precious. ..(1 Peter 2:7a)

Thank You, Lord God, for circumstances that have propelled me into a deeper relationship with You. Thank You for those who insisted I learn how to seek Your face. Thank You for Christians who knew of the excitement of daily growth, daily surrender, daily prayer, and daily obedience, and didn't give up on me. They observed me as I lived a mediocre life as a Christian. They cared enough about me and about the kingdom of God that they persisted in telling me how to worship, learn, and study in meaningful ways.

O God, we in the body of Christ must awaken to our responsibilities. You give us new life daily that we may share it daily. We seek Your face in order that we may grow in grace and in the knowledge of You. Give us the willingness and the urgency to share with others.

You supply this loving grace to be shared in the world. Lord God, help us be bold, courageous, and humble enough to care about helping the body of Christ to grow. Transform us until we become vulnerable for Your cause. Help us all speak Your truth as we hear the prompting of Your Holy Spirit. Help us all to be honest to the point of being rejected for Your sake. Help us to love relentlessly to the point of being misunderstood.

Because of the bold witness of long ago Christians who took their responsibilities seriously, I began to do the things that would help me find more of You. Today I am walking through valleys that I didn't know existed. Because Christians cared enough to help me learn how to grow, I seek You daily, and You help me stand in victory. You have become so precious to me! Help me, to the point of being vulnerable, to help others. In Jesus' name. Amen.

"And let him who thirsts come.
Whoever desires, let him take of the water of life freely."
(Rev. 22:17b)

The Offending Rock

...but to those who are disobedient, "The stone which the builders rejected has become the chief cornerstone," and "a stone of stumbling and a rock of offense." They stumble, being disobedient to the word, to which they also were appointed. (1 Peter 2:7b-8)

Good morning, Lord. Thank You for being attentive to my heart, my concerns, and my entire life that I am trying to live for You. It is more than I am able to comprehend. I sit at Your feet and worship You, almighty God. Thank You for the sacrifice of Your Son, Jesus. Thank You that He bore my sins in His body on a tree that I might be forgiven and born into this newness each day. Teach me true worship as I bow before You.

When those of us who believe consider those who continue to reject the chief cornerstone, we wonder at the power of pride that refuses to be humbled. This spirit today is evidenced when powerful minds, full of knowledge, become puffed up. Head knowledge refuses the idea of total submission to You, Lord, and pride rears its ugly head in rejection. Our hearts puzzle over the stone that the builders have rejected throughout the history of our world. We wonder at the power of pride that allows truth to become a stone of stumbling and a rock of offense.

How can we in the body of Christ share with others the joy that comes from obedience to You? Your will runs counter to modern teachings of self-sufficiency and self-determination. Your teachings disagree with the modern idea that humans have everything they need within themselves to conquer any obstacles in life.

We cannot share Your truths without Your wisdom and Your special anointing. It is Your anointing that breaks barriers and offers life. So we humble ourselves before

Chapter Two

You in worship—great God, our Father; Jesus, our Redeemer; and the Holy Spirit, our promised Comforter and Guide. We wait before You today, precious Holy Trinity. Speak to our hearts anew. Help us convey the message of the cross to those who are perishing. Make foolish the wisdom of this world through us as we attempt, with Your grace, to bring Your powerful message to the world. In Jesus' name we pray. Amen.

"That He might sanctify and cleanse her [the Church] with the washing of water by the word."
(Eph. 5:26)

Special People

> But you are a chosen generation, a royal priesthood, a holy nation, His own special people, that you may proclaim the praises of Him who called you out of darkness into His marvelous light...
> (1 Peter 2:9)

Precious Father and my God, I greet You today with a heart full of praise. Thank You for time that I'm able to use any way I choose. I choose to spend time with You, holy Father. I choose to lift my heart and hands in submission to Your command that we proclaim Your praises.

Thank You for calling us Your chosen people, and thank You that all have the opportunity to choose You. I have become a part of this chosen generation, Your royal priesthood, and Your holy nation. What a glorious truth!

Thank You for calling us Your "special people." You give us Your beautiful and welcome command to be faithful to the call to praise You. Thank You for continually wooing the world by Your Holy Spirit, drawing all of us to accept Jesus as Messiah and Lord of our lives. O Lord, who are we that You should want to bless us so in this life and offer eternal life through Jesus? This truth causes praise to well up and spill over! Help us to let our joy spill over into meaningful relationships.

Not only have You called us from darkness into Your marvelous light, Your light seems to illuminate more and more as we proclaim Your praises. Illuminate our lives today that others may be drawn into becoming a part of Your chosen generation, Your royal priesthood, Your holy nation, Your special people.

We want to be used for Your glory. O God, thank You for the reality of living in this marvelous light. We pray in the precious name of Jesus, our Lord, our Savior, and our Redeemer. Amen.

Chapter Two
Mercy

> *...who once were not a people but are now the people of God, who had not obtained mercy but now have obtained mercy. (1 Peter 2:10)*

Today is overcast Father; it reminds me of my life before I turned it over to You and began to walk in Your light. My days were purposeless, sometimes dark and dreary. You tell us in the verse above that at one time we were not Your people, but now we are the people of God. We need to be reminded often about the difference in our lives. The gulf between darkness and light is great, and we should not let one day go by without rejoicing in our new life.

Because of Your mercy that gives to everyone the gift of faith, we can have the assurance that we are a part of Your people, for we were chosen and called. Because of Your hand of mercy, we responded to Jesus. Thank You, Lord, that Your mercy is everlasting and Your truth endures to all generations.

You saved us because of Your mercy by allowing Your Son to die in our place. Thank You for the bond of fellowship established with Jesus through His shed blood and the spiritual bond the blood establishes between believers.

Remind us often of the time when we were not Your people, the time when we had not yet obtained mercy. And in this reflection, sweet Jesus, cause our hearts to burst forth with grateful praise! We praise You, merciful Father, Son, and Holy Spirit. Amen and amen!

Sojourners

Beloved, I beg you as sojourners and pilgrims, abstain from fleshly lusts which war against the soul... (1 Peter 2:11)

Most holy and precious Father in heaven, I bow humbly before Your throne of grace this day. As I contemplate Your words of truth, I feel a stirring deep within my heart. You have special plans for the body of Christ. You are doing a work across our nation in the hearts of Your people. Instill in us all that our hearts are able to receive. Help us become more receptive, malleable, and contrite.

Forgive me for my errant ways and restore a right spirit within me. Help me follow Your commands today. Recreate Yourself within me that I might be the beacon of light You intend all Christians to be in this world.

As I think of the weaknesses of my flesh, I heed the words of the apostle Peter to abstain from fleshly lusts—these deceptive desires that do war against my soul. My mind, will, and emotions are susceptible to the daily temptations of this life. Only You, by Your Spirit, can make me aware of these deceptions.

Bring me into an acute awareness of sin today, Father, and bring me to genuine repentance that I become the obedient sojourner and pilgrim You want me to be. I want to fulfill Your purpose for my life as You continue to bless me with days on earth. Fill them with Yourself, blessed Lord, and I shall praise You continually. Help me stay in the shadow of Your wings today. I love You, Lord, with all my heart. In Jesus' name. Amen.

Chapter Two
Victory Over Evil

...having your conduct honorable among the Gentiles, that when they speak against you as evildoers, they may, by your good works which they observe, glorify God in the day of visitation. (1 Peter 2:12)

Holy Father, precious are these times set aside to come into Your refreshing presence. You are a miracle-working God when I spend time thinking upon Your words. Oh how wondrous is Your love for humankind! I reach out, and You are there when I take Your commands to heart. My heart tells me Your commands belong to me personally. Thank You for blessing me with Your miraculous touch.

We come with empty hands today, so fill them for Your glory. Dear Lord, because of Your touch we have every confidence that our conduct among those who do not believe will meet with Your approval. How thankful we are for Your fortifying presence! You bring to nothing the evil that may come against us. There are those who deny our Lord and Savior by hurting Christians with their words. These hurtful words could destroy if it were not for Your power at work in us.

As Your witnesses, we choose to bless and not retaliate. As Your blessed children, we seek to have peaceful and humble spirits. As Your disciples, we rejoice in the knowledge that You are our defense, and we do not return evil for evil.

Remind believers everywhere to continue in good works and powerful words of love in the presence of evil. Help us help those who do not believe. We give all glory to You, Lord, when You touch others through us. All honor and glory belong to You—Father, Son, and Holy Spirit. Thank You for continuing a miraculous work in our hearts. In the precious name of Jesus we pray. Amen.

Submission

Therefore submit yourselves to every ordinance of man for the Lord's sake, whether to the king as supreme, or to governors, as to those who are sent by him for the punishment of evildoers and for the praise of those who do good. (1 Peter 2:13-14)

Dear Lord, will I ever stop battling against submission? I think not! Over and over again, You must teach me it is in submitting to necessary circumstances that You make me strong. Yes, I want to be an overcomer, but it is so difficult to yield to all the circumstances You place in my life.

I yield to my spouse according to Your divine order, I yield to everyday rules and regulations set by governing authorities, and I yield to most situations as I walk through a day's activities in my life. It is difficult, however, to yield to repeated, unfair treatment for Your sake. Help me. Give me patience. Touch my pain.

You suffered wrongfully, Lord Jesus. You were accused, spat upon, suspected of treason, and questioned constantly by those who loved You and those who despised You. Yet out of obedience to Your Father, You always conquered through quiet strength. Your words of wisdom brought victory to every situation.

Let me be reminded of Your obedience to Your Father when I am tempted to rebel and say words against those in authority who may use their power wrongfully. Thank You for Your Word instilled in my heart so long ago: "Whatsoever you do, do it heartily as unto God and not unto man" (Col. 3:23 KJV). Your command is a challenge and not easy to follow. Sometimes my flesh rules, and I cause You grief. Forgive me my trespasses!

Strengthen my resolve to submit myself to every ordinance of man for Your sake—whether to kings as supreme, or to governors, or to those who are sent by You for the punishment of evildoers and for the praise of those who do good. Help me pray for those in authority and do good at every opportunity today, for I know this is always Your will. I pray in Jesus' name. Amen.

"And let him who thirsts come.
Whoever desires, let him take of the water of life freely."
(Rev. 22:17b)

Doing Good

For this is the will of God, that by doing good you may put to silence the ignorance of foolish men... (1 Peter 2:15)

My Father and my God, in the midst of clutter, in the midst of demanding lists, good intentions, necessary appointments, and the daily need to prioritize, I come to You. Thank You for being my haven of rest and my peace. I look to You for strength and stabilization. Gather my thoughts as I rest in You.

Father, I'm feeling the unrest of our world and the uneasiness and uncertainty of our future. Only You can calm the heart and reassure the soul. Come into my heart, Lord Jesus, with Your comforting presence.

Already Your Word has spoken deeply to me. You have quickened my inward person. Thank You for Your healing touch. Precious Lord, I give thanks to You. I lift my heart in praise to You. I rejoice in the newness You recreate daily when I look to Your Word and lean upon You. I lean upon You heavily today, precious Master. Give me the willingness to do good in the midst of busyness. Help me think of others and their needs. Make my prayers more sincere and my deeds more Spirit-directed.

It seems the world is bent upon bringing dishonor to You and Your servants. Anoint our deeds and good works. Do help us continually examine our motivations for good works. Cleanse our hearts so that all we do will reflect Your love and sincerity. With Your direction and Your special touch, we will silence the slander and foolishness of those who have not tasted Your goodness. Increase our love for the world of the unsaved and unenlightened. In this increase, You will be glorified. All honor and praise to You, almighty God! We pray in the name of Jesus. Amen.

Chapter Two

Use of Freedom

...as free, yet not using liberty as a cloak for vice, but as bondservants of God. (1 Peter 2:16)

O Lord, how wonderful is the freedom You give me to walk in Your love! How amazing is this process of sanctification that continues to increase my freedom. Thank You for warning me about the dangers of increased freedom. You tell us our enemy walks about, stealthily seeking whom he may devour. He is bent upon corrupting and destroying this increasing freedom that God's children enjoy. He comes at us in various, devious ways. He often tries to make us feel too deeply satisfied. In our satisfaction he takes great delight when we avoid the discipline of spending daily time in Your Word and prayer.

I bask in this freeing liberty with You, Lord. In my exuberance the temptation is at times strong to do or say things that might be misunderstood by others. So help me avoid carelessness in my witness. Help me be sensitive to the needs of those around me. This joy and freedom in You is so glorious, but without the wisdom that only You can provide, it could become a stumbling block that would keep another brother or sister from experiencing more of You.

Remind me again of the bondservant relationship with You. Once again I bind myself to You and Your love. Remind me that Your love is not offensive. Your love is patient, gentle, good, and always empathetic. Prevent me from using the liberty You give as a cloak for wrongdoing, but let it bind me ever closer in my daily commitment to love others. I pray in Jesus' name. Amen.

Honor People

Honor all people. Love the brotherhood. Fear God. Honor the king. (1 Peter 2:17)

Father, Your commandments are demanding but wise and life-producing. You command us to honor all people by showing respect to the lowly, loving the unbelievers, and giving our attention equally to all people You bring into our lives.

My old nature encourages me to favor those who favor me. My old nature helps me ignore the undesirables in the world and turns my attention elsewhere. Help me give due respect in all encounters throughout this day. Help me dispense Your light wherever I go. Give me an awareness of Your desires, so that I give a welcoming smile, an encouraging word, a helping hand, or a listening ear to all.

Lord, You know my need for patience. Forgive me for making excuses for bad behavior. Instill in me Your peace that will cause me to wait upon You. In this waiting, create patience in me to honor everyone with listening ears and help me to feel the heart needs of others.

Thank You for those enlisted in leadership everywhere. Impress the seriousness of responsible leadership upon those who influence our children, youth, and adults. You command us to honor all leaders. Help us pray for our leadership. We should not concentrate on their faults but pray for them out of love for You, Lord. Bless our country and strengthen the body of Christ to become all that You would have us to be. Especially help us all to show honor to each other, so that Your kingdom will come on the earth. In Jesus' name. Amen.

Chapter Two

Submission

Servants, be submissive to your masters with all fear, not only to the good and gentle, but also to the harsh. For this is commendable, if because of conscience toward God one endures grief, suffering wrongfully. (I Peter 2:18-19)

*O*Father, the misuse of power in so many ways has become a familiar problem to us all. What causes those who have authority to abuse others? I think of Christians using their wonderful freedom wrongfully. What is it in our flesh—our sinful nature—that causes us to put others down and lift ourselves up? With amusement I recall the response of one believer to this question: "Meanness!"

Help us, Lord, to grow in fear of You, for with our increased respect of You, we also grow in our respect for humankind. Help us see others as precious souls, tender souls that need to be treated with the same awesome respect with which we have learned to treat You.

Father, today I lift to Your throne of grace all those who have employers that are harsh and disrespectful in demeaning ways. Help employees return good for evil and positive words for unfair words. Help the mistreated have a pleasant attitude in response to the bullying, deceiving, and unfair acts or power plays that take advantage of those who are in serving positions.

You assure us that returning good for evil will bring eventual victory in Your eyes. It is for Your sake that we put up with unfair treatment. You tell us You are pleased with us when, for the sake of conscience, we patiently endure unfair treatment. So help us show respect to everyone with whom we come into contact this day. In the name of Jesus we pray. Amen.

Patience

For what credit is it if, when you are beaten for your faults, you take it patiently? But when you do good and suffer, if you take it patiently, this is commendable before God. (1 Peter 2:20)

Father, it is such a privilege to greet You each day. Thank You for watching over me this past week. I've been aware of Your gracious provision day after day. You give me clarity of mind when I need it most. You give me extra energy when I feel weary from the stress of caregiving. You give comfort to my soul when outwardly everything seems crazy. You steady my feet when I begin to doubt and wonder. Your presence is like a healing balm in the midst of man's disapproval and, sometimes, harsh words.

Lord, Your Word tells me to take responsibility for my faults. You say that I do not deserve credit for taking rightful criticism patiently. How clearly that teaches I must take responsibility for my wrong behavior! Thank You for helping me to recognize the error of my ways. Thank You for Your patience in dealing with me. This process of growth seems so slow at times, and continually I try to release the reins of my life to You. I trust Your love and faithful concern.

Your command is to always do good, and sometimes we are criticized for doing good things for others. This helps me begin to realize what believers are called to become. When I do good, I may suffer for it, but I must take it patiently—this and only this will bring Your commendation. I like the clarity of Your teaching. Help me to become more like Jesus. Give me the strength and desire to see myself as I truly am. In Jesus' name. Amen.

Chapter Two

The Call

For to this you were called, because Christ also suffered for us, leaving us an example, that you should follow His steps... (1 Peter 2:21)

Lord God, this is another splendid day You have created, and I will rejoice and be glad in it. Thank You for the lovely dawn and the beauty of Your creation. It's a pleasure to breathe in the earthy smells of the dawn and the newness of the day. Thank You for Your promise that You are the same yesterday and today; You will be the same always. You are worthy to be praised, O Lord, and I magnify Your holy name! Heaven and earth reflect Your glory. Heaven and earth praise You.

Your Word is a hard word today, Lord, as You tell me I am called to suffer as Christ suffered for me. Is this what You are saying to me—that one aspect of suffering is being treated unfairly when I am trying to live a life of doing good? In my humanness I want credit and praise for doing good. But You tell me, as a Christian, I am called to do good and suffer just as Christ suffered for mankind, leaving us an example to follow.

Help us all understand more fully the true meaning of suffering for our faith. Lord, as we endeavor to relate to You and surrender our hearts to be crucified for Your cause, I am beginning to understand more and more what it means to follow in Your steps. Help me to consider suffering as a privilege. Open our hearts to understand the many glorious shades of suffering for Christ. Thank You that out of this obedience to Your Word, You tell us our suffering will bring great glory and unexplained joy. Thank You that Your promise to us is that You will take us from glory to glory. We praise You, almighty God. In Jesus' name. Amen.

Deceit

> *...who committed no sin, nor was deceit found in his mouth... (1 Peter 2:22)*

Father, You tell me that my Lord and Savior, Jesus Christ, committed no sin, and no deceit was found in His mouth. What a challenge to my heart as I contemplate these truths! According to Your Word, I should be changed day by day into Jesus' likeness. Your promise to me is that I will be transformed into the same image from glory to glory by Your Spirit (see 2 Cor. 3:18). I accept Your condition to this promise that I am to live by the truth of Your Word and under the influence of Your Holy Spirit.

Thank You for the high expectations You have for us. Thank You for the sanctifying presence of Your Holy Spirit who helps us daily to see these high expectations as opportunities for growth and not demands from You.

This life is glorious when I am able to let Your Spirit lead and guide me. When Your Spirit controls my life, I have great love for others, and You free me from sin and deceit. Father, this deceit is so subtle and tries to work in my life in so many ways. Remind me, Holy Spirit, when I am tempted to tell partial truths, bend the details of events, stretch the truth, or commit the sin of deceit by not speaking when words are needed. Father, keep me aware of the need for transparency before You and before others so that my life will glorify You. Help me in my weaknesses. In Jesus' name. Amen.

Chapter Two

Commitment

...who, when He was reviled, did not revile in return; when He suffered, He did not threaten, but committed Himself to Him who judges righteously. (1 Peter 2:23)

Lord God, it amazes me as I think upon Your Word day after day and see the depth of its meaning that can be applied to our lives. Since I have come to know You, I have assumed the position that Christians sometime suffer as Christ suffered. The full meaning of this truth and its application to my life has been difficult to fully comprehend.

My understanding of submission and its relationship to suffering is slowly penetrating deep into my heart. You lay a beautiful groundwork in First Peter for me to draw upon by telling me to lay aside my flesh and grow in You. Then You go into detail about Jesus' being the "chosen stone." After that, You explain why we are a chosen generation, a royal priesthood, and a holy nation; and You remind us that we are called out of darkness into Your marvelous light. We are to be a proclaiming people who live in high praise.

After laying that foundation of truth, You tell us that we are called to suffer as Jesus suffered. Jesus is our example. Thank You, Lord, for Your unmistakable explanation of suffering. You go on to explain that Jesus was reviled, berated, and criticized, that He suffered, was exploited, oppressed, and used as a scapegoat. He never retaliated nor did anything to gain revenge. That is suffering!

Thank You for these hard but clear teachings about how believers are to live in this world. We are so privileged to be Your children. But with these privileges come Your high expectations. Forgive us when we fail You, and we do at times. Help us strengthen our commitment to

You, and enlighten all of us to the seriousness of our high calling. In Jesus' name. Amen.

"That He might sanctify and cleanse her [the Church] with the washing of water by the word."
(Eph. 5:26)

Chapter Two

Dead to Sin

Who Himself bore our sins in His own body on the tree, that we, having died to sins, might live for righteousness—by whose stripes you were healed. (1 Peter 2:24)

Thank You, Lamb of God, for the open invitation to come to Your throne of grace. How special it is to experience the wonder of Your love day after day—this love that welcomes me gladly, enfolds me, and keeps me in tender care!

Father, some days I come wounded, weary, and beaten down because of the cares, doubts, fears, and the strange happenings in our world. But I come now into Your presence, knowing that You, and only You, can heal and restore me to wholeness again.

Thank You, Lord Jesus, for bearing my sin in Your own body on the tree, so that I could die to sins and live for You. Thank You for giving me the power to resist sin and live in the Spirit. As I think upon this truth that lies at the center of my faith, it overwhelms me. You bore my sin on the cross that I would be called daily to die to my self-centeredness. You call the body of Christ to recognize the beautiful challenge ever before us—to become more and more like You. In Jesus' name. Amen.

Prodigals

For you were like sheep going astray, but have now returned to the Shepherd and Overseer of your souls. (1 Peter 2:25)

Father, this verse reminds me of the parable of the lost sheep. Your search for every lost sheep extends to all of mankind. Your compassion expressed in the parable of the lost sheep extends to all the lost children of the world. You do not want any to perish, and Your offer of eternal life is for everyone who will acknowledge Jesus Christ as personal Lord and Savior.

O God, how I praise You for Your Holy Spirit who continues to draw everyone toward You! I pray today for those who are being spoken to in Your still, small voice. O Father, quicken ears to hear You today. Use Your people to witness to others who are in valleys of indecision. Give us courage and the grace to speak to those who are searching. Temper our witness with Your caring compassion, and then the lost will be drawn toward the Shepherd and Overseer of their souls.

Keep us ever mindful that we, too, were like straying sheep until You spoke to our hearts. You spoke through Your people, by Your Holy Spirit, through circumstances, and through believers who were bold enough to love as You would have them love.

Remind us again and again of what life was like without You. Let gratitude move us toward a lost people with the fire of Your love. In Jesus' name. Amen.

Chapter Three

Adaptations

Wives, likewise, be submissive to your own husbands, that even if some do not obey the word, they, without a word may be won by the conduct of their wives... (1 Peter 3:1)

Thank You for my husband, Lord, and the biblical pattern for marriage given to us in the Word. Submitting to my partner is a difficult, daily learning experience. Adjusting to a constant willingness to honor him sometimes fights against my flesh. My old nature wants to control instead of exercising a quiet and gentle spirit.

Again and again You teach us that when we are yielded to You, we are yielded to life situations. You tell us rebelliousness is as the sin of witchcraft (1 Sam. 15:23), so help me cultivate that quiet and gentle spirit that releases more understanding and goodness in my husband.

Again and again I seem to need reminders that it is in adaptation and adjustments that I become victoriously stronger. Thank You, Lord, that through this yielding and adapting to life situations, You do make me stronger. In Your strength, growing in holiness becomes true reality. Becoming more like Jesus is another lesson in suffering—difficult but glorious.

Temper my voice today and add Your compassion and gentleness to those situations in which I become impatient and my anger wants to flare. Help me pray for my husband in difficult situations so that Your hands are free to work for Your purpose and glory. Father, when I pray for more love and patience, You do relieve the stress and lighten my load. Prayer is submission. Prayer shows my willingness to grow in holiness and in respect for my husband. Keep me mindful of the place of authority that You've ordained for him in our marriage.

Keep me through Your power as I walk in obedience to life situations. Especially I thank You for daily lessons that I learn through trying to be the partner and follower You want me to be. The struggle is exciting, Lord, for it is with Your strength that I walk and await, through faith, my salvation that is ready to be revealed when Jesus comes. I pray in Jesus' name. Amen.

"And let him who thirsts come.
Whoever desires, let him take of the water of life freely."
(Rev. 22:17b)

Chapter Three

Chastity

...when they observe your chaste conduct accompanied by fear. (1 Peter 3:2)

Father, I rejoice in these quiet, holy moments when worldly cares are shut out, and You hold me close to Yourself as I wait upon Your presence. The quietness of the early hour with You is precious and awesome.

I lift holy hands in honor of Your holy presence. Speak to my heart and prepare me for the day. Let Your living presence wash away the debris of ugly thoughts, negative attitudes, troublesome memories, or anxious cares that profit no one. Search my heart and show me those distasteful traits that become evident in the light of Your love.

What a challenge it is to consider Your command that my conduct become chaste for Your glory! Only You, by Your Holy Spirit, can mold my conduct day by day into this pure image. Purify my conduct, cleanse my motivations, and cause my behavior to improve day by day, Lord Jesus. I cannot improve my behavior on my own, but with Your help and the prompting of Your Holy Spirit, my conduct will slowly become molded according to Your will.

Thank You for a healthy fear of the Lord, which is a gift from You. I tremble in Your presence, not because I am frightened, but because of Your holiness. I give You highest honor this day. I worship You and am devoted to fearing You. Revive me anew in Your righteousness. I trust in Your Word, which is impregnated with Your presence and illuminated by my Helper, Your precious Holy Spirit. I pray in Your name, precious, holy Jesus. Amen.

Influence

Do not let your adornment be merely outward—arranging the hair, wearing gold, or putting on fine apparel... (1 Peter 3:3)

Father God, I think of all the attitudes in our society that influence my thoughts, and I know I'm not immune to forces all around me. I too focus on my appearance and wonder how others perceive me. Too often I'm influenced by vanity and the norms of society.

Forgive me for being overly concerned about the clothes I wear and how I look. Thank You for reminding me that man looks on the outward appearance, but Your concern is with the condition of my heart. Help me center my thoughts upon Your earthly kingdom and help me order my days according to Your plan for my life.

Give me wisdom for these days. I know my outward appearance is another way to attract unbelievers to You. So help me choose modest but becoming apparel. I manicure this body and keep it clean for Your glory. Help me to be adequately enough "in style" so that I will not distract another that might be weighing my witness.

Keep me in a good balance, Lord. Save me from unnecessary distractions like arranging the hair, wearing gold, or putting on fine apparel. Center my thoughts and my purpose for living on You and the needs of others around me. Again and again You show me how Your abundant grace and wisdom flows when I'm looking outward, away from myself.

I desire to reflect You in this world, so touch my heart anew today, sweet Jesus. In Your name I pray. Amen.

Chapter Three

Gentleness, Quietness

> *...rather let it be the hidden person of the heart, with the incorruptible beauty of a gentle and quiet spirit, which is very precious in the sight of God.*
> *(1 Peter 3:4)*

This is Your day, sweet Jesus. How thankful I am that You awakened me with a song in my heart! The song was put there by You several years ago when Your Holy Spirit touched me, and I made You Lord of my life. When I awaken, the song is there. As I walk through the day, it is there. When the day is done, it is there. I love You, my Lord, my strength, my rock, my fortress, my deliverer.

Thank You, Lord, for the power of Your Word that affects my attitude. I think about the miracle of change, which You, by Your precious Holy Spirit, cause to take place in human hearts. The power of Your presence working through Your Word is truly miraculous. After spending time with You, I feel revived, and the song is more distinct.

You come in and remold us day after day because we are receptive and because You love us. Thank You for love that will never let us go! You tenaciously hold us to Yourself, even when we are not so lovely. My heart is hidden except to You, Lord. You are aware of my many secrets, and nothing is hidden from Your sight.

I surrender myself anew to the lofty goal You have for all Your children—that of a quiet and gentle spirit which is precious in Your sight. My Father and my God, create in me a beautiful, gentle, and quiet spirit. Mold me day by day as I attempt to live for You. Empower me as Your witness and move me through today under the influence of Your Holy Spirit. In Jesus' name. Amen.

Holy Women

For in this manner, in former times, the holy women who trusted in God also adorned themselves, being submissive to their own husbands...
(1 Peter 3:5)

Precious Lord, the sun is shining so brightly today. Feeling its warmth is like basking in the warmth of Your love. This season is rich with the evidence of creation all around. The miracle of new life is springing up from the ground; this seems a parallel to new life You bring to human hearts.

Warm me thoroughly today, sweet Holy Spirit, that my life might brush the lives of those who don't know You. Make me more aware of longing, searching hearts. Help me have a gentle, quiet spirit like the holy women of former times. In this gentle love and quiet witness, You will mold and make me to make a difference in our world. Touch others through me, gentle Holy Spirit, as You touched and continue to touch through the lives of Your saints of old and saints who walk the earth today.

Thank You, Lord God, that an understanding of submission begins with You, and You help me live this victorious submitted life in every circumstance. Thank You, Lord, for my spouse whom You've taught me to honor more and more with each passing day. And thank You for my spirit, which is growing in gentleness and quietness as a result of this submission. Your Word truly lights my understanding daily, and it is a lamp to guide my feet wherever You lead me.

Daily I want to walk in submission to You, Holy God, and with Your help, I will live a submitted life on this earth—submitted to my spouse, to our circumstances, and to the authorities whom You've appointed to rule in all places. Thank You, Lord, that in my willingness to live this yielded life, Your grace is sufficient for me, and my strength is made perfect in weakness. In Jesus' name. Amen.

Chapter Three

Role of Women

> ...as Sarah obeyed Abraham, calling him lord, whose daughters you are if you do good and are not afraid with any terror. (1 Peter 3:6)

*W*e are living in times of anxiety, Father, and our whole country realizes that America is no longer the safe haven it once was. Terrorists abound within and without our country, and their threats are very real. We look to You, O Lord, as our glory and our shield. Thank You that many are crying out to You in these distressed times and many are being saved.

Raise up wise leaders in our world who will work together against evil forces. Thank You for awakening the body of Christ to the real task set before us—to represent You in the earth. O Father, strengthen us! Lift up the light of Your countenance upon us and put within us new gladness and resolve to be Your hope in our anxious world.

In Your Word, You remind women to be obedient to husbands, just as Sarah of old obeyed Abraham, calling him Lord. That is still a word for us today. You are still calling us to authenticity as daughters of Abraham. What a noble calling and challenge! You call us to be as those having an unfading loveliness with calm and gentle spirits.

Remind us again that it is in eager submission to You, O Lord, that we find ourselves free—free to live a life of submission, free to love and respect others as we love You. In this desire to give ourselves to You daily, without reservation, we are no longer encumbered with threatening feelings that hinder our submission to others and life's situations.

I pray for all women, and I pray for myself. Help us all find that noble strength, those calm and gentle spirits of the women of old. We take delight in You, Father.

Mold us and make us the strong leaders and counterparts for our husbands that You intend us to be. We rejoice in knowing that You hear us. In Jesus' name. Amen.

"That He might sanctify and cleanse her [the Church] with the washing of water by the word."
(Eph. 5:26)

Chapter Three

Heirs Together

Husbands, likewise, dwell with them with understanding, giving honor to the wife, as to the weaker vessel, and as being heirs together of the grace of life, that your prayers may not be hindered. (1 Peter 3:7)

Father, when I think of "being heirs together of the grace of life," I realize that You give such fullness to that phrase. Not only are married couples heirs together of the grace of life, but Christian brothers and sisters are also to live together in that same harmony.

Man has tried to make new rules to this grace of life and Your Word, but Your will and Your instruction are the same today as they were yesterday and will be forever. You tell us that women are physically weaker as You created us with this submission in mind. Teach us again and again, holy Father, that we can find our strength in obedience to Your Word.

I glory in Your truth that my spouse and I are equal heirs to the grace of life when we honor and obey You for in this honor and obedience, we hold each other in the highest esteem. In this obedience to You and honor for each other, competitiveness is resolved and middle walls of partition between partners disappear (see Eph. 2:14).

Even though, as my husband's caregiver, our roles have somewhat reversed, You still keep my respect for him constant, and I'm thankful. Keep me in this obedience for it reaps a peace that can only come from You.

Thank You for the assurance that You are hearing our prayers. Thank You for Your precious Holy Spirit who confirms our faith and confidence that we are heirs together of the grace of life. In Jesus' name. Amen.

Compassion and Tenderness

Finally, all of you be of one mind, having compassion for one another; love as brothers, be tenderhearted, be courteous... (1 Peter 3:8)

What powerful words You have given us in I Peter 3:8—compassion, tenderheartedness, courteousness! These are the attributes we are to extend to the body of Christ and the world.

I'm so grateful, Father, for the love and compassion extended to us in my husband's illness. There are days we seem so needy; many times it's on these very days that others stop by or call. Their love and compassion is a tender touch from You. It kindles our hope and brings reality to Your love working through the body of Christ.

We are called to extend these attributes to all, and what a calling this is! You tell us in Galatians 6:2 to carry one another's burdens to fulfill Your law, but how can we possibly carry the burdens of others if we are not caring, compassionate, tender, and courteous? We cannot!

We need your help, Father. Strengthen our weak arms that hang down. Increase our desire to extend Your love and understanding. Make us courteous toward those who are treating others badly. Increase tenderness and compassion in our hearts so we will make a real difference in someone's life today. Put such a call to evangelism upon all our hearts that we will be drawn boldly toward those who have not yet accepted You as King of kings and Lord of lords—the Creator of the universe.

We look to You for strength. Without You, we can do nothing, but with You all things are possible. In Jesus' precious name we pray. Amen.

Chapter Three
Called to Bless

...not returning evil for evil or reviling for reviling, but on the contrary blessing, knowing that you were called to this, that you may inherit a blessing. (1 Peter 3:9)

Lord, You tell us not to return evil for evil. Evil takes so many different forms. We are living in days when man seems to have become more tolerant and yet more self-centered. Tolerance seems to be a license for accepting immorality; and in this downward spiral of acceptance, man has become so much more insensitive to his own accountability.

Forgive me, Father, when I make excuses for others and for myself—that is the way of the world, and You exhort me to be in the world but not of it. I want to be accountable to You, Lord, and to what You expect of me as Your child. I want to return good for evil. Help me live in this world in such a way that I will be a blessing and will inherit a blessing in the future life. Let Your Spirit of wisdom so rest upon me that when evil is thrust upon my life, I will respond with Your love and compassion.

What a challenge it is when You command us to return blessing for the many forms of evil that might be done to us. Thank You that we are called to inherit the blessing of eternal life. And out of obedience, Lord, I thank You that I have Your call upon my life to return good for evil. Thank You for an increasing strength that comes from You each time I obey this call.

Your commands are hard, but in You and through You, You make it possible to live according to Your Word. Thank You for giving me the desire to obey and thank You for the many blessings that result from obedience. In Jesus' name. Amen.

The Tongue!

For "He who would love life and see good days, Let him refrain his tongue from evil, and his lips from speaking deceit. (1 Peter 3:10)

Father, I have become more aware of the unruliness of my tongue at times in recent years. Thanks to You, Holy Spirit, I do come under conviction when my behavior is displeasing to You. I create a negative or positive atmosphere in our home with the words of my mouth. How easy it is to give in to my fatigue and let impatience take over! Lord, forgive me for sharp words, self-pity, or saying careless or harsh words that vent my distress but injure others.

You give me a wonderful formula for good days and a lovely life: "Let him refrain his tongue from evil, and his lips from speaking deceit" (I Pet. 3:10b). I know it doesn't matter what the situation, when I take Your Word as my individual instruction, You bless my going out and my coming in with Your precious presence. The closer I walk with You, the more I love life and have victorious days.

Father, help me have good days. Prepare my heart with Your Word today that I might not sin against You. Let Your Word so prepare me that my tongue will speak pleasant words, sweet to the soul and health to the bones (see Pr. 16:24).

Lord, I cannot will myself to refrain my tongue from speaking evil and my lips from speaking deceit or untruths. Help me. Touch my mouth again and again with the fire of Your presence, precious Lord. Burn away tendencies toward deceit and words of the tongue that do not reflect Your heart.

As I get to know You better and fall deeper and deeper in love with You, I trust that You will keep my tongue from evil and cause my lips to speak more truth. I have faith in Your desire to give me the desires of my

Chapter Three

heart, so I'm thanking You in advance for a day full of rich experiences, filled with love and positive words. Thank You for guarding my mouth so that I will reflect You in what I do and say. Thank You for Your Son, Jesus, in whose name I pray. Amen.

"And let him who thirsts come.
Whoever desires, let him take of the water of life freely."
(Rev. 22:17b)

Church Transgressions

Let him turn away from evil and do good; Let him seek peace and pursue it. (1 Peter 3:11)

Thank You, O God, that You sent Your Son, Jesus, to die for our sins. He is our perfect role model in this life, and His words speak wisdom and instruction that no one could ever duplicate. His actions were always gracious and merciful; He was slow to anger, and His steadfast love abounded to all. Is it any wonder that we, as Christians, are instructed to ask ourselves when confronting situations, "What would Jesus do?"

Father, You command us, as Your children, to turn away from evil. What kind of evil? Too often, we attribute evil to those things going on outside the church family. It is easy to point beyond the church walls and assume it's not too difficult to stay away from the obvious sins of pornography, gambling, fornication, prostitution, drinking, and the like. Help us understand Your commands are for the Church!

As realistic Christians, we must admit that we sometimes exercise competitiveness, verbal control, envying, jealousy, unfeeling responses to need, disdain for the less fortunate, corporate and personal pride, and selfishness in the body of Christ. And this list is far from complete. Isn't this relative to the words of Jesus when He told us to worry about the log in our own eye before we become too concerned with the speck in our brother's eye? (See Matthew 7:3.)

Father help us, as Your church, to seek Your mercy continually. Wash us thoroughly from our sins and help us recognize our many transgressions. Help us turn away from evil and concentrate on doing good for Your sake. Help us live lives of repentance so we can be used to help grow Your earthly Kingdom. In Jesus' name. Amen.

Chapter Three
Ears and Eyes

For the eyes of the Lord are on the righteous, And His ears are open to their prayers; But the face of the Lord is against those who do evil. (1 Peter 3:12)

What precious promises You give us in Your Word today! You tell us that Your eyes are upon us, and You call us righteous. Me—righteous? I sometimes struggle with the word righteous. Somehow it is difficult to accept that You call us righteous simply because of our faith in Jesus Christ and our acceptance of Him.

Through faith I have come to know You, Jesus, the power of Your resurrection, and the fellowship of Your sufferings. Through my faith and Your grace, I am becoming conformable to Your death. Thank You, Father God, for transferring the righteousness of Jesus Christ to those who trust in Him.

I trust You, Jesus. You are the Messiah. You are all truth—the Lamb of God and Bishop of my soul. I'm so thankful for the blessed day when I surrendered to Your Lordship and made a radical commitment to allow You to be my anchor and way of life.

Your Word tells me Your ears are open to my prayers. O Father, what a marvelous revelation from You when I began to accept all that Jesus did for me on the cross of Calvary! I come daily to You now through the blood of Christ. I am washed whiter than snow because of the blood of Christ. I am cleansed from sin and made whole. I am redeemed through Jesus' blood.

Indeed, I offer prayers to You through the blood of Jesus, and because of His blood, You hear me! Help me share the excitement of my faith with others today. With Your help, I will help others. In Jesus' name. Amen.

Doing Good

> And who is he who will harm you if you become followers of what is good? (1 Peter 3:13)

Hear my voice, precious Lord, as I lift holy hands to praise You. I see Your faithfulness and sovereignty daily as the dawn arises. What glorious beauty I have to enjoy! Keep me from taking Your provision for granted and deepen my appreciation of earth's splendor.

I draw nearer to learn more about You this morning, precious Savior. The words from Matthew 11 come to my mind when I think of a relationship with You: "Take my yoke upon You and learn of Me." Gladly I take this yoke upon me. My desire to learn more of You is a beautiful gift. Thank You for this yearning that causes me to seek You day after day.

Will anyone harm me if I'm doing good? My first response is to say, "No one, Lord." Indeed it would be rare if I were to be harmed while attempting to do good. Sometimes I might think I am doing good when, in Your eyes, my motivation may be wrong. Help me examine my heart and motivation for doing good. Forgive me when I do good for special attention. Create in me a servant's heart, one that will put the welfare of others before myself.

Teach us to pray before we act. Teach us to listen to Your still, small voice. Teach us to question our motivations as churches, as individuals, and as the body of Christ. And Lord Jesus, give us the willingness to repent when You reveal our selfish, self-centered motivations. Thank you for loving us in our weaknesses. In Jesus' name. Amen.

Chapter Three

Threats

But even if you should suffer for righteousness' sake, you are blessed. "And do not be afraid of their threats, nor be troubled." (1 Peter 3:14)

Indeed, O Lord, it is a small thing to be persecuted for Your sake. Even now as I think of the life of my precious Savior, I bow my knees and cry, "Holy, Holy is the Lord who died for my transgressions." Precious is the blood that was shed for my sin. Only the blood of the innocent Lamb of life could pay the price for my sins and the sins of the world.

Thank You that God Himself set the pattern of restitution for sin when He slew an innocent animal in the presence of Adam and Eve as payment for their sin. Thank You for the clarity of Your Word and for Your Holy Spirit who gives us understanding of its meaning for us today.

O Lord, help me count it as privilege and blessing when I see the world coming against the children of God. Remind me that "The Spirit of glory and of God rests upon us" when this happens (see I Pet. 4:14). Help me praise You when the war between good and evil accelerates on so many levels—our home, community, city and state governments, and especially between our political parties and our branches of government.

Threats are increasing to the body of Christ as definitions and doctrines are being twisted to suit the whims and gainful intentions of man. O Lord, do have mercy on us. Forgive our selfish motivations, and restore integrity to the body of Christ and to the entire leadership of our nation.

Because of the daily strength You give me, I shall not be afraid of threats or troubled by rumors, Lord. You created me, and You call me by name. I belong to You. As I am passing through troubled waters, You are with me.

Rivers of fear cannot overwhelm me because You are in control of my life and the life of our nation. Thank You, my Lord and my God, Holy One of Israel and my precious Savior. Amen.

"That He might sanctify and cleanse her [the Church] with the washing of water by the word."
(Eph. 5:26)

Chapter Three

Our Responses

But sanctify the Lord God in your hearts, and always be ready to give a defense to everyone who asks you a reason for the hope that is in you, with meekness and fear... (I Peter 3:15)

Father, how mysterious and yet exciting is the word "sanctify"! It seems that it has only been in small degrees, as I travel along on the continuum of life, that I am gradually grasping and experiencing sanctification. I'm not satisfied to accept a brief definition of it. You are so much larger than that, Lord. Let Your creative revelation flow as believers are faithful to spend time with You in Your Word!

Wash me daily with the water of Your Word as I bow my knees and cry, "Holy, holy, are You, oh Lord, Author and Finisher of my faith. I praise Your holy name. Sanctify me with Your truth, and Your Word is truth (see John 17:17).

Fill my heart with truth so I'll be able to share with everyone who might ask, the reason for the hope that is in me. Because it is a lifetime process, I ask for Your help daily. I belong to You. Now mold me and make me after Your will.

Speaking for You is an awesome responsibility, so fill my cup that I might have words to defend and postulate my faith and hope in You. You tell me to do this with meekness and fear, so I lean heavily upon You, dear Lord, to fill my mouth when opportunities arise to share a word about Your greatness in my life (see Mt. 10:19-20).

You are Lord of lords, our High Priest, the Living Water and Bread of Life. You are Prophet and King, our Redeemer and anchor when the troubles of this life seem insurmountable. We serve You in meekness and fear. Gift us with this inner strength. We lift Your name on high. In Jesus' name. Amen.

Clear Conscience

...having a good conscience, that when they defame you as evildoers, those who revile your good conduct in Christ may be ashamed. (1 Peter 3:16)

Good morning, Lord. Last night before I went to sleep, Your presence surrounded me; and again this morning when I awakened, Your presence blessed me. Thank You for a good night's rest. Thank you for a good conscience that allows good rest. I am not without faults and problems, yet You stabilize me. My days are often stressful as constant caregiver, yet I am aware that I'm standing on the Rock. I need You every hour, Lord Jesus, and I thank You for Your peace in the midst of turmoil.

All You have said in previous verses: "Turn from evil, sanctify the Lord God in your heart, do good and seek peace," if obeyed, help give me a good conscience. A good conscience produces good works and good words that will affect the enemy.

Thank You for building sensitivity within that allows me to know in my heart when I'm walking with You and when I'm walking without You. It's me, Lord, who walks away from good conduct, so keep me close to Yourself today. I want to be fortified against the enemy by not only having a good conscience but also by having good conduct.

You tell me that if I keep my conscience clear, it won't matter if my reputation is defamed. Evildoers who revile and persecute cannot overcome Christians. You will have the victory always, and those who persecute and defame character will be ashamed because of the evidence—our good works and good conscience that speak Your wisdom and concern for others.

Father, I'm remembering Your Word that put me on shouting ground in a time of unfair, inflicted pain: "If you are reproached for the name of Christ, blessed are you,

Chapter Three

for the Spirit of glory and of God rests upon you. On their part He is blasphemed, but on your part He is glorified" (I Pet. 4:14). Help me, Holy Spirit, to do a good work today and ever keep my conscience clear for Jesus' sake. In His name I pray. Amen!

"And let him who thirsts come.
Whoever desires, let him take of the water of life freely."
(Rev. 22:17b)

Suffer for Good

For it is better, if it is the will of God, to suffer for doing good than for doing evil. (1 Peter 3:17)

Lord God, as I dwell in 1 Peter 3:17, the phrase, "if it is the will of God," causes me to wonder about Your will. Jesus didn't do anything without Your approval, and He walked continually in Your will. What an example for me to follow!

Suffering for Your sake is a part of the commitment I made when I decided to become Your disciple. Help me better understand what a privilege I have in You to suffer for Your sake.

This relationship with You as Your disciple reminds me of other earthly relationships. I made a commitment to be a helpmate to my husband. That commitment has involved hardship, tough decisions, and much sacrificial living. Yet I count it all joy as You have taken a governing role in that commitment. I made a commitment to be a mother. Again, that commitment to motherhood has involved suffering as well as blessing. Even my commitments to my neighbors and other friends cause me hardships at times, but I know this suffering is a result of doing good.

For some time now I have committed myself to be my husband's caregiver. This is Your will, and although it involves much hardship, I have the assurance that it is Your perfect will. You are doing a work in me that I do not fully understand, but it is peaceful to be walking in obedience. There are days when I feel discouraged and wonder, "How long?" but when I lean more heavily upon You, there is relief, and I feel assured that all is well. Your peace passes my understanding.

Truly I count it all joy when hard times come while serving You, whether the hardships have come while serving as wife, mother, or caregiver. There seems to be

Chapter Three

no separation in these roles for all is done for Your glory. What a privilege to serve You in every way! In Jesus' name. Amen.

"That He might sanctify and cleanse her [the Church] with the washing of water by the word."
(Eph. 5:26)

Dead Flesh

> For Christ also suffered once for sins, the just for the unjust, that He might bring us to God, being put to death in the flesh but made alive by the Spirit... (1 Peter 3:18)

Precious Jesus, forgive me for studying Your Word without taking the time to praise You. When I think of all You've done in my life, it seems a small thing that I should not be singing Your praises from morning to night.

You found me! Rather, I should say, I found You when I reached the end of myself. I was floundering, lost, bewildered, unsettled, aimless, and lifeless. I responded to You, and You saved me. You, in Your boundless mercy, saved me. What a change began to take place in my life, and what a miraculous process is the continuing change! I praise You, Almighty God, and I thank You for Jesus, the perfect sacrifice, who suffered and died for my sins that I might live a heavenly life while still living on this earth. Hallelujah!

Thank You for the "Just One" who died for all the unjust that we could be reunited with our Creator. What a small thing it is, then, to suffer in this life as Your disciples, that we might be a part of drawing others to You. Keep us authentic in this commitment to carry out the Great Commission (see Mt. 28:18-20).

Thank You for the apostle Paul who considered the sufferings he endured not worthy to be compared with the glory that would be revealed in himself (see Ro. 8:18). He identified our sinful flesh when he described himself as wretched, having good and evil warring within himself (Ro. 7:23-24).

Just as Jesus was put to death in the flesh that He could carry the burden of sinful humanity, so we put our flesh (our sinful nature) to death. Then we are quickened (made alive) by Your Spirit and can make a difference in

Chapter Three

this world! Let it be so, precious Jesus. In Your name I pray. Amen.

"And let him who thirsts come.
Whoever desires, let him take of the water of life freely."
(Rev. 22:17b)

Called to Preach

...by whom also He went and preached to the spirits in prison... (1 Peter 3:19)

Thank You, Father, that today is another brand new start. When I view Your creation—the earth, the skies, the warmth of Your sunshine, and the birds singing heartily—I pause to express gratitude. Thank You for who You are. Thank You for all You've created for our pleasure.

Yesterday is gone, but my heart is singing the new song You give me for this day. Let that song so resonate that imprisoned souls are drawn into that blessed hope You give to the world. Just as this miraculous hope is an extension of my faith—help me declare (preach) this precious hope to others. I want to be Your channel today. Give me the courage to take opportunities in my path.

Open my eyes to see and hear the silent cry of imprisoned spirits all around. Help me declare Your love. O Father, forgive me for taking responsibility too casually. You call us all who have been born again to preach Your Word, and this surely means to declare its truths daily.

Your concept of sanctification builds within us a good conscience, and Your concept of suffering makes us more and more alive in the Spirit as we suffer for Your sake. Help us appreciate the freedom that grows in our lives as we are made more and more alive by Your Spirit. Compel us, Lord, to share that freedom with others.

Your Spirit has been made alive in us because of the cross. Now, O Lord, help us in our calling to reach out to those who are in the valleys of decision—imprisoned spirits we come in contact with in our daily lives. We have many opportunities to plant seeds and expand Your earthly kingdom. Help us take those opportunities that Your will be done now as it shall be in heaven. In Jesus' name. Amen.

Chapter Three

Jesus' Longsuffering

> ...who formerly were disobedient, when once the Divine longsuffering waited in the days of Noah, while the ark was being prepared, in which a few, that is, eight souls, were saved through water. (1 Peter 3:20)

Father, last night was difficult. I'm so in need of a refreshing touch from You. You are my refuge, my high tower, my dwelling place. I anticipate Your embrace as I sit before You with arms opened wide.

I extol You, my God, O King—I will bless Your Name forever and ever. You sent redemption to Your people; You cause my heart to be steadfast. I'm so thankful that my heart is established in You. Come, Holy Spirit, bathe me in Your soothing presence.

Father, Your Word is so revealing and powerful when I let You speak to me as You spoke to Your children through the Apostle Peter. How patient You are and have been with humankind. Your Holy Spirit waited and wooed disobedient children for 120 years while Noah was building the ark; only eight souls listened to the wooing of Your Holy Spirit.

In light of Your longsuffering, it must be foolish to ask myself, "How long should I pray for a lost soul? How patient should I be with those who continually reject You? How patient must I be with the world that rejects everything I stand for because of You?"

This instructs me as Your follower toward the real meaning of patience, obedience, and Jesus' longsuffering. Forgive me, Lord, for my impatience with those who seem to have no interest in Christianity—those who stubbornly refuse the wooing of Your Spirit. Keep me faithful to pray for lost souls. In Jesus' name. Amen.

Buried With Jesus

There is also an antitype which now saves us—baptism (not the removal of the filth of the flesh, but the answer of a good conscience toward God), through the resurrection of Jesus Christ... (1 Peter 3:21)

Precious Jesus, thank You for the privilege of addressing You today. And I thank You for allowing me to address all parts of the Trinity for You are one, and there is no separation of the Godhead. How thankful I am for the warmth of the Father's love, the model of Jesus for my behavior, and the constant guidance of the Holy Spirit.

There is so much confusion taught today about baptism when Your Word tells us it is a symbol of salvation to be understood according to our faith. Only Your Word can explain baptism accurately, and no one denomination or group has a corner on the interpretation of Your Word.

Thank You for the vivid experience of baptism. How breathtaking were the waters when I was immersed! The cooling, cleansing, refreshing experience underscored my desire to die to myself and live for You. As I came up out of the water, I knew in my heart that I had arisen to a deeper life of obedience that could be likened to Jesus' own death and resurrection.

Thank You for the joy that floods my soul today when I recall that day of celebration. I was buried with Jesus through baptism into death and raised from the dead by the glory of the Father. Continue to crucify my old nature as I attempt daily to walk in newness of life with the clear conscience You provide through the washing of Your Word. Hallelujah to the Lamb of God! In Jesus' name. Amen.

Chapter Three

Our Great Intercessor

...who has gone into heaven and is at the right hand of God, angels and authorities and powers having been made subject to Him. (1 Peter 3:22)

Thank You for this early morning hour before my husband arises when I can spend precious time with You, Lord Jesus. How delightful the quiet. How delightful when You suddenly give new understanding to Your Word. How reassuring when You bless me with Your surrounding presence. Encompass me anew, Holy Spirit, as I wait upon You.

O Father, how reassuring it is to know that when I come to You in prayer, I am reminded again and again that Jesus always lives to make intercession for me. I have Your Word that tells me He sits in heaven at Your right side, intervening on my behalf. For this reason, I pray for myself and for others with great confidence, knowing that my great Intercessor is also pleading my cause.

I lift the loved ones and friends You have caused me to remember to Your throne of grace. I seek Your intervention on their behalf. Bring them the peace that passes all understanding and ignite their hearts with the flame of Your reassuring love. Your ways are not our ways, and we often do not understand the miraculous responses to our prayers, but we thank You for them.

Most of all, dear Lord, I thank You that Jesus sits at Your right hand, interceding for His children in power, as angels and authorities and powers are under His command. What a privilege to carry everything to You in prayer! In Jesus' name. Amen.

Chapter Four
Fellowship of Suffering

Therefore, since Christ suffered for us in the flesh, arm yourselves also with the same mind, for he who has suffered in the flesh has ceased from sin... (1 Peter 4:1)

I glory in Your precious presence this day, Lord God. Just when I feel that You are not so near, You bless me by surrounding me with Your Holy Spirit. My finite mind wonders how this blessing of Your presence is possible all over the world. Many believers are experiencing the same glory. Thank You for inhabiting Your Word and the prayers and the praises of Your people. Truly You are doing new and wonderful things upon the earth!

You tell me to arm myself with Your mind, and in this preparation I shall be better able to understand and enter into the suffering of Jesus. Help me lay aside my own desires for worldly recognition so I will grow in faith to know Jesus and the power of His resurrection. Help me enter into the fellowship of His suffering. Then I will better understand His mind and grow to become more like Him.

Enlarge my understanding of how suffering for Jesus' sake will give me greater strength to resist the temptation to sin (see I Pet. 3:18). Thank You for the reminder that all unrighteousness is sin (see I Jo. 5:17). Move me closer, Lord Jesus, to You. Help me have the willingness to die to my own desires and live for others.

I pray this prayer with great excitement and trust in the work You are doing in the body of Christ. In Jesus' name I pray. Amen.

Chapter Four

God's Will

> *...that he no longer should live the rest of his time in the flesh for the lusts of men, but for the will of God. (1 Peter 4:2)*

Again and again, precious Jesus, I am reminded of the importance of living with praise in my mouth throughout all of my days. Forgive me for those times when I fail to acknowledge You; I do this when all is going well. I praise You for the glorious splendor of Your majesty, Your wondrous works, the might of Your awesome acts, and the way You satisfy the desire of every living thing.

I praise You for the dawning of this day, the beauty of the rose-colored sky, and the early morning quietness that invites You to come in. Thank You for filling this quietness with Your very presence. I sit quietly and absorb Your life-giving touch. Truly You are my all-in-all, and I praise Your holy name.

Oh, Father, that we would spend less time discussing praise and more time praising You! Forgive the Church (all of us) for continually missing the mark. Help us realize that when each of us hungers and thirsts for more of You, our churches will come alive with praise.

Thank You, Holy Spirit, for helping the Church live, not according to the guidance and recommendation of men, after the flesh. Help us all to avoid self-centered thinking by submitting our wills to You and then following Your leading. We need Your constant reminder that Your Word is Your will. We praise You, most holy God, Holy Spirit, and Jesus, our Brother and our Friend. In Jesus' name I pray. Amen.

Our Past

For we have spent enough of our past lifetime in doing the will of the Gentiles—when we walked in lewdness, lusts, drunkenness, revelries, drinking parties, and abominable idolatries. (I Peter 4:3)

Thank You, Lord, for reminding me of the way I lived before I accepted You as my Lord and Savior. Before this change took place, I lived my life for me. My life was all self-indulgence and self-preservation. I spent my time doing and accomplishing everything I could for my own sake.

Your will seemed like a distant idea that would be good to follow, but in all probability, unattainable. Lord, You call that kind of living, "living in the flesh and living for the lusts of men." Now I know my life was just the opposite of living for You, and I was far from living in the will of God.

How beautiful is this life in the Spirit that I live now! How exciting is the knowledge that I am being changed day by day into Your image! Early in my walk with You, that idea seemed impossible. But now, as I grow in my devotion to You, as I arm myself daily with the mind of Christ by spending time in the Word and in prayer, this concept has become an everyday reality. Truly Your will is Your Word, and I cannot know Your will without reading Your Word and talking with You.

So wash away the debris of yesterday. Forgive my trespasses as I forgive others. Fill me today with Your purpose for me in this life. Lay out the plan for my day. Open my ears to hear and my eyes to see all You want me to do. And, Lord, supply the love and grace it will take to accomplish all You want done. I pray these things in the precious name of Jesus. Amen.

Chapter Four

Remembering Our Past

For we have spent enough of our past lifetime in doing the will of the Gentiles—when we walked in lewdness, lusts, drunkenness, revelries, drinking parties, and abominable idolatries. (I Peter 4:3, repeated Scripture)

Thank You, Lord, for another day, rich with expectation. Thank You for a night of peaceful rest because of Your presence. Help me to live this day in Your love and grace, for I want to do Your will. Quicken my heart today so that I am willing to give for the welfare of others.

You remind me, Father, of the former years of my life when I did the will of the world. I need this reminder, for the memory of my former life seems so distant and easy to forget. How selfish and self-centered I was in those days of blindness!

Thank You for invading my life so long ago. Thank You for the gradual transformation of my mind, will, and emotions that has become a precious and real process. Thank You for the washing of the water of the Word and for Your Holy Spirit that helps me interpret that Word.

Thank You for prayer that continues to bring change to my heart. Lord, I'm Your "work-in-process." How vibrant and unshakable is the faith in my heart that You will complete Your good work. Continue to change my old nature so that I become more and more at home in Your will.

I am far from Your goal of perfection, but I'm also far from living the life I used to live. Thank You for this glorious life in the Spirit. Keep me close to Your heart today that I might not sin against You. In Jesus' name. Amen.

Caregiving

> *In regard to these, they think it strange that you do not run with them in the same flood of dissipation, speaking evil of you. (1 Peter 4:4)*

Father, thank You for the daily peace You give me in caregiving. Thank You for keeping me from falling into depression and self-pity. Because You hold me in the palm of Your hand, I have beauty where there could be ashes and the oil of joy that replaces the tendency for mourning. How comforting to know You will and do meet me in deepest need!

There are, however, the hard times when I wonder if I'm going to have the wherewithal to carry on, and You send a friend, a relative, or we receive a telephone call or special mail that lifts our hearts to a higher level. Father, how we thank You for angels who come in so many forms when we are so needy.

You speak of the former life when I might have run in "the flood of dissipation with other unsaved souls." Thank You for the Hound of heaven who caused me to live in unrest and lack of peace when I was younger—that is until that glorious day You touched me and when peace flooded my soul.

If the world should reject me or "think me strange" for loving You, that's all right as I no longer need the world's approval—I'm living for You as the center and purpose for my existence. Doing Your will keeps me busy, and I'm no longer affected by the way our archenemy works through the unsaved.

Help me stay in close relationship with You, ever mindful that the enemy of our souls prowls around seeking whom he may devour (see I Pet. 5:8). In Jesus' name. Amen.

Chapter Four

Judging Others

They will give an account to Him who is ready to judge the living and the dead. (1 Peter 4:5)

Father, You are teaching me about the fine line between evaluating and judging. My human nature is too quick to judge. This is wrong as You tell me everyone will give an account to Him who is ready to judge the living and the dead.

Thank You, Lord, for confirming to my heart that all judgment is Your responsibility. You tell me not to war with another, but to love, edify, and build up the body of Christ in positive ways. Thank You for the way believers are used for Your purposes, even when our motives are not all that You want them to be.

Make me more aware of opportunities to build up my brothers and sisters in Christ. Help me see in others the ultimate purpose You have for their lives. Most of all, dear Lord, help me to both rejoice when others rejoice and relate to them in their times of need so they will yield even greater increase for Your glory. I pray these things in the precious and mighty name of Jesus. Amen.

God Equips

For this reason, the gospel was preached also to those who are dead, that they might be judged according to men in the flesh, but live according to God in the spirit. (1 Peter 4:6)

Lord Jesus, thank You for Your Word that teaches me all truth. My soul waits upon You this day, for in this expectancy, my hope will be rewarded. In this time of waiting, connection is made in my heart from the earthly to the heavenly. In this time of waiting, instruction is given, and Your precious peace fills my heart.

Thank You for Your peace that passes my understanding and from which my confidence arises. As I continue to make Your commandments my delight, You fill me with Your Spirit, equip me for Your work, and fill my mouth with praise. Thank You for inhabiting the praises of Your people.

With Your equipping I am able to proclaim Your Gospel today with confidence. With confidence in You, even the hard shells of skeptics will be shaken, and Your Spirit will impact lives. I shout praises to the glory and power of Your name.

O Lord God, help me be a witness of the Gospel to those whose spirits are dead, and let Your words, through me, bring life so they too will begin to live according to Your Spirit. In Jesus' name. Amen.

Chapter Four

Watchful Prayer

But the end of all things is at hand; therefore be serious and watchful in your prayers. (1 Peter 4:7)

Lord Jesus, You call me to daily prayer, but I struggle, often forfeiting this wonderful privilege to be blessed. Your Word commands us to praise without ceasing, so help me keep my mind and heart focused on You.

Forgive me for the days I shorten my devotional time, sometimes skipping the praise You so justly deserve. Forgive me when I treat prayer and intercession lightly, for I know in my heart You dispatch angels to respond to the prayers of Your children.

You tell us the end of all things is at hand, so cover our nation's leadership with the blood of Jesus, strengthen them, and make them more cognizant of Your desire to intervene in the affairs of men. Thinking men and women know that terrorist activity is increasing all over the world. Give us the wisdom to recognize potential trouble and give us the courage to report it to proper authorities.

Forgive us for our fear of making mistakes and give us the courage of our convictions that we might better serve You and our country. Help us appreciate and guard our freedom in You. Again, Lord, forgive and cleanse us of careless prayer lives, for through prayer You give us boldness and courage. Now help us be more serious and watchful. In Jesus' name. Amen.

Warm Love

And above all things have fervent love for one another, for "love will cover a multitude of sins." (1 Peter 4:8)

O miraculous, wonderful, and magnificent God—You who know all hearts inside and out; who knows all things from the beginning to the end, how do I approach You who rule the universe? My heart is full of wonder and awe. I wait. And then, Lord, I believe I hear Your still, small voice beckoning all believers and unbelievers alike, saying, "Come! Just come unto Me."

So I come, just as I am, expressing my gratitude for the honor and privilege of speaking so intimately to One who loves me so personally. You are so much more than I am able to comprehend. I rejoice in Your love for humankind. I rejoice in Your open arms. Your invitation is for all of us to simply come and talk with You.

Just as You love without reserve, so too You command us to love without reservation. Fill us with Your eager, tender love that overflows and covers our sins. Help us love the unlovely, the burdened, the apathetic, the uncaring, the despicable, the mean and miserable, and the despondent. Help us love obediently so greater love might be birthed in us for each other and the world.

This agape love that You give, precious Father, absorbs rejection. It reaches through dislike and rebuttal in order to reach out eagerly to the one who doesn't know You. Truly Your love is warm, strong, empathetic, and expressive. This warm love is compassionate and reaches out to the sinner; it endures for others and overlooks their faults. Help us love like this. In Jesus' name. Amen.

Chapter Four

Happy Hospitality

Be hospitable to one another without grumbling.
(I Peter 4:9)

Father, I quiet myself before You this morning and await Your presence. Thank You for this precious time to spend with You. I halt the clamor of my thoughts that tumble about me, for it is in my deliberate effort to quiet myself before You that You are able to penetrate this unrest and equip me for another day.

Thank You for this silence and the miracle of Your soothing presence. A calm is filling me as I sit quietly and simply desire to worship You. I hear Your heavenly music in my heart as I await Your presence. Truly Lord, I lift Your name on high.

Your Word tells me to be hospitable, without grumbling, and that truth continues to multiply in my heart. I so much admire those who have the gift of hospitality, and I observe the ease and joy with which they open their lives and homes to welcome others.

Hospitality without grumbling is doing for others lovingly with pleasure in our hearts. What a gift! And what a joy to see this gift working in the body of Christ, not just for Your children, but also for those who do not know You. Thank You for the stories of hospitality I read in Your Word that continue to teach the real meaning of willingly doing for others.

Create in me, O Lord, a hospitable heart. Bring things to my mind today that will help others. And fill my heart with joy in the doing that others will be blessed. In Jesus' name. Amen.

Gifts

> As each one has received a gift, minister it to one another, as good stewards of the manifold grace of God. (1 Peter 4:10)

Daily I turn to You, precious Lord, in gratitude and thanksgiving. How wonderful are your provisions for humankind! You gave us Your very self so that we could see the image of God, our Father. You surrendered Your life on the cross that we might be reconciled to God and one another. You laid down patterns for us to live by in all that You said and did while You walked and lived among us. And now we have Your provision, the precious Holy Spirit, our Comforter, who is leading and guiding us into all truth.

O Lord, my God, how magnificent is Your name in all the earth! You set Your glory above the heavens. Indeed when I consider the heavens, the work of Your hands, the moon and the stars that You have created, I live in awe of You. I serve an awesome God!

In all Your gifts and manifold goodness to me, let me not forget to praise You always. Help me use Your gracious bounty to build the body of Christ. Increase gratitude in my heart so much so that I become consumed in serving You by serving others.

Remind me again and again that success in anything I am, anything I have, and anything I hope to be, lies in my willingness to use the gifts to benefit others. I surrender all and look with heightened expectancy to a day rich with Your guidance. Come, Holy Spirit. I need You and Your direction today. In Jesus' name. Amen.

Chapter Four
Ministry

If anyone speaks, let him speak as the oracles of God. If anyone ministers, let him do it as with the ability which God supplies, that in all things God may be glorified through Jesus Christ, to whom belong the glory and the dominion forever and ever. Amen. (I Peter 4:11)

Father, the richness of Your Word continues to astound me as I meditate in it. You have commanded me to meditate in it day and night as You command all Your children to do (see Josh. 1:8). How little we partake of Your holiness through the Word when You offer it as a constant flowing well for our edification!

You tell those who speak, to speak as the oracles of God. We cannot speak with effectiveness unless we have spent time with You. You tell us to minister as with the ability that You supply. The phrase "as with" tells me to be constantly aware of gifts and abilities that become effective for You as You receive credit for everything. Keep reminding me, dear Lord, that You supply gifts to Your children so the work of Your earthly Kingdom may be accomplished.

Gift me today that I might speak and minister for You. Be glorified, Father, through Jesus Christ, to whom belongs the glory and dominion forever and ever. You alone are worthy to be praised. In Jesus' name. Amen.

Understanding Trials

Beloved, do not think it strange concerning the fiery trial which is to try you, as though some strange thing happened to you... (1 Peter 4:12)

Lord Jesus, the more I learn of You and obey Your commands, the more I understand the forces at work against Your will coming to pass on the earth. Early on in my walk with You, it seemed amusing when I heard saints speaking of "walking through fiery trials," but little by little, these trials have begun to unfold in my own life.

Thank You for helping me understand the life You want me to live as I walk through my days here on earth. Without You and the gifts You supply as well as the trials, where would I be? I would be moving in my own strength, accomplishing very little for You, and existing in an aimless, selfish vacuum, without the daily touch of Your Holy Spirit.

My heart cries along with that of David, and I, too, say, "O Lord, take not Your Holy Spirit from me" (Ps. 51:11), for I cannot live, I cannot do right things, speak truth or write truth without You, precious Holy Spirit, my Guide, Counselor, creative power and wisdom! (See Mark 13:11; Rom. 14:17; and Pet. 1:12.)

Most of all, precious Master, I ask You to continue to allow trials in my life, for in these trials I learn to depend on You. Forgive me when I complain—and I do complain sometimes. Thank You for Your mercy. I praise You for Your greatness. You alone are worthy to be praised. In Jesus' name. Amen.

Chapter Four
Enter Into Suffering

...but rejoice to the extent that you partake of Christ's sufferings, that when His glory is revealed, you may also be glad with exceeding joy. (1 Peter 4:13)

Lord Jesus, I take joy in the expectancy of seeing Your face at that time when Your glory is fully revealed. In the meantime, Lord Jesus, I take pure joy in Your love daily; I bathe in the glory of Your presence and the gentle touch of Your Holy Spirit. How precious is this time of waiting upon You! Thank You for the joy of expectancy and the excitement of Your daily infilling.

I feel like the psalmist David when he said, "A day in Your courts is better than a thousand. I would rather be a doorkeeper in the house of my God...You are a sun and shield and will give grace and glory..." (Ps.84:10a, 11c).

This concept of suffering is elusive. As I relate to Jesus, as I allow God to expand me, as I continue to see things from His point of view, I get glimpses of what it really means to suffer. When my heart aches for the lost and disillusioned, when I weep for those who war against each other in the name of Christianity, and when I long for His kingdom to come on earth, then I begin to understand minutely why happiness flows from afflictions.

Father, I count it all joy to serve You. Help me remain faithful until Jesus comes, then I shall be "glad with exceeding joy!" In Jesus' name. Amen.

America's Freedom

If you are reproached for the name of Christ, blessed are you, for the Spirit of glory and of God rests upon you. On their part He is blasphemed, but on your part He is glorified. (1 Peter 4:14)

Father, so many forces of evil are at work both in and out of the body of Christ today. Give Your people wisdom to realize the many reproaches against us are often concealed under the guise of doing good things for our nation and our world. How subtle is the evil one!

Help us have hearts that will hunger after Your wisdom that we might stand in peace and strong in might against evil forces. Evil does takes its stand, at times, in the hearts of men who govern the laws of our land, those who create policy for our educational institutions, and those who make rules for our fields of science, health, and technology.

Lord, attract many Christians, who are strong in faith, to participate in these important areas. Awaken us to the responsibility we have for the direction of our country and world. Indeed, You have commissioned us with the Great Commission given to all those who are willing to take Your yoke upon themselves. To those of us who are willing, you give the same authority when You command us to "make disciples of all nations, to baptize, to teach and observe all Your commandments for You are with us always, even to the end of the age" (paraphrased Mt. 28:19-20).

Give us courage in these days to cease indulging in excessive tolerance. Give us boldness to stand fast in the liberty and cause to which You've called us. Keep us ever aware of the insidious bondage that will result if we do not guard our minds and souls with diligence. The welfare of the body of Christ is threatened. Our country's

Christian freedom and heritage is under attack. We need You in this hour. In Jesus' name. Amen.

"That He might sanctify and cleanse her [the Church] with the washing of water by the word."
(Eph. 5:26)

Personal Behavior

But let none of you suffer as a murderer, a thief, an evildoer, or as a busybody in other people's matters. (1 Peter 4:15)

This morning I stood and looked out the kitchen window at daybreak. Breathtaking! Time seems to stand still as the wonder of it registers in my heart afresh. Thank You, Lord, for Your faithfulness. You bless me with the privilege of awakening to another day of sunshine, birds singing, shimmering dew, and gentle breezes. I pause and try to take it all in—life is so rich and so good because of You.

As I consider the suffering of Christians written about by the great apostle Peter, help me realize the importance of my personal behavior. He speaks of suffering unnecessarily for wrong behavior such as thievery, any kind of evildoing, and even acting as a busybody in other people's matters.

I could easily say I don't do any of those things. But wait. I believe, above all things, that Your command is for Christians to lead lives of doing good. So if we suffer, it should be for doing good, not for those things we are apt to do when behaving carelessly.

Lord, Peter made it very simple when he said, "If you are going to suffer, let it be suffering which comes from serving God." Help me mind my own business today, and at the same time, be actively concerned in serving others. I give You all of my heart, soul, and mind. Use me for Your glory. In Jesus' name. Amen.

Chapter Four
Self-Will

Yet if anyone suffers as a Christian, let him not be ashamed, but let him glorify God in this matter. (1 Peter 4:16).

Father, today promises to be another busy day. I pause, breath deeply, and attempt to quiet my heart before You. Numerous and difficult tasks lie before me; I do not want to approach them without Your enabling grace.

Forgive me for racing through some days without asking for Your help. When I neglect You and the help You offer, relying on my own self-sufficiency, I always make a mess of things. Thank You for another hard lesson learned because of my disobedience. I've wasted Your time and missed opportunities for witness because of my stubbornness and self-will.

Your instructions about suffering are clear. You tell me to always let You lead, and I will have no reason to be ashamed when life is hard. If I'll do this, I can readily glorify You in all things, no matter what. Forgive my sin, and set my feet on the right path today. My life is Yours. Mold me according to Your glorious hand. It's in the precious name of Jesus, I pray. Amen.

Believers' Judgment

> For the time has come for judgment to begin at the house of God; and if it begins with us first, what will be the end of those who do not obey the gospel of God? (1 Peter 4:17)

My Father and my God, I need Your help for the problems that are weighing so heavily upon my heart today. I take these burdens and place them upon You. Forgive me for allowing the heavy load to keep me from communion with You. Thank You for Your patient waiting for me to let go completely so You might fill my heart with peace.

You help me realize Your peace that passes my understanding. By faith, I receive that peace so Your hands are free to work in every area of my situation. Fill me now as I look to You, in trust, for I need You in this hour.

In Your Word You tell us that the righteous will scarcely be saved (1 Pet. 4:18). That seems to cancel any thoughts one might have about judging an unrighteous world, for You want us to leave judgment in Your hands. You tell us the time has come for judgment to begin with Christians so we must be concerned with our personal relationship with Jesus Christ, as well as with one another.

I pray that the Gospel of Christ will take more and more preeminence in my daily living. Thank You, Lord, that You love me enough to remind me that judgment begins with the house of God. Your patience with the human race is long, enduring, and compassionate, because You long for all of us to come to repentance.

Show me again the areas in my life that need refining and give me the courage to willingly repent. I need the refining of Your Holy Spirit since the time has come for judgment to begin at the house of God. In Jesus' name. Amen.

Chapter Four

Saving the Righteous

Now *"If the righteous one is scarcely saved, Where will the ungodly and the sinner appear?"* (I Peter 4:18)

Great are You, O Lord, and greatly to be praised! Thank You for another day to serve You. In these days of unrest I thank You that You still reign on the earth. Your promise to us is that the earth is firmly established and cannot be moved. You, Lord, are most high above all the earth, and we exalt You far above all gods.

Father, as I mull over the judgments in Your Word, I consider Peter's claim that the righteous will "scarcely" be saved. Lord, this does not provoke fear in my heart, but it increases the seriousness of keeping my heart right before You.

I remind myself that no one has known or will know the mind of the Lord, and none shall ever become Your counselor. All things are of You, through You, from You, and return to You.

Thank You, Lord, that Your Word gives understanding to know right from wrong. Thank You that Your Word guides us, judges us, and enables us daily. You give us wisdom and prudence through Your Word. Keep us faithful to read it and meditate on it daily so that Your Holy Spirit, step by step, might guide us throughout our days.

Keep us faithful to pray for ourselves, the ungodly, and sinners, as we know Your will is that none should perish. Help us to cooperate with Your Holy Spirit so hearts will be touched, turned, and saved according to the lifetime salvation plan You have for all our lives. Thank You again, Lord, for we are so privileged to be a part of Your earthly work and the increase of Your Kingdom. In Jesus' name. Amen.

Doing Good

Therefore let those who suffer according to the will of God commit their souls to Him in doing good as to a faithful Creator. (I Peter 4:19)

Father, I come as Your child today. Thank You for the privilege of turning to You in praise and thanksgiving. Thank You that Your ways are beyond my own feeble understanding, but the privilege of seeking You and learning of You remains an exciting and rewarding pursuit. My ongoing relationship with You never stops growing.

Thank You for the wisdom You have provided in Peter's writing and for the lovely, practical picture he paints regarding suffering. Through serving in goodness, day after day, I experience the reality of suffering. And in this reality, I experience more grace and glory because Your Holy Spirit rests upon those who walk under the influence of Your leadership.

Thank You for Your faithfulness as my Creator; I see daily evidence of Your creative work on the earth. I commit my soul to You and look forward to experiencing the results of walking in Your will.

Fortify me today with Your love and grace so that I may bring the light of Your glory where there is darkness and despair. I am humbled in Your presence, sweet Savior. Thank You for the honor of carrying the light of Your love to others today. I pray these things in the glorious name of Jesus Christ to whom belongs all honor and glory forevermore. Amen.

Chapter Five
Motivators

> The elders who are among you I exhort, I who am a fellow elder and a "witness" of the sufferings of Christ, and also a partaker of the glory that will be revealed... (1 Peter 5:1)

O Father, how I thank You for the brotherhood of Christ. What joy this fellowship, and what strength I receive from others! Whether it is worship, Bible study, telephone communications, or chance meetings, the oneness in spirit enriches my days. Thank You for the abundant life in Jesus Christ and the joy of becoming a part of the family of God.

Thank You for calling those who are more experienced in service to be exhorters (motivators and encouragers) to the younger members of the body of Christ. Forgive me for the times I fail to motivate others, and in that encouraging, build up my brothers and sisters. Forgive me for failing to acknowledge needs when You reveal them to me. Take me beyond my own immediate needs. I want to respond to the needs of others.

O Lord, You are aware of every Christian's work performed in Your name. You are aware of every labor of love we show to others for Your sake. We count on Your goodness, Your fairness, Your justice, and Your mercy, for You promise Your children that You will not forget any action performed for Your cause.

You instruct mature Christians to exhort (motivate and arouse) others in the body of Christ so they become excited about serving. You tell us this is the way to understand the sufferings of Christ and become partakers of the glory that will be revealed (see I Pet. 4:13). Help us walk actively in the light. Let us be so enthusiastic about our living for You that we become a contagious witness to the world. Help us, like Peter, to become exhorters, edifiers, and loving witnesses for Your Kingdom. In Jesus' name. Amen.

"And let him who thirsts come.
Whoever desires, let him take of the water of life freely."
(Rev. 22:17b)

Chapter Five

Leading Others

> ...Shepherd the flock of God which is among you, serving as overseers, not by compulsion but willingly, not for dishonest gain but eagerly... (1 Peter 5:2)

Father, as we sing to Jesus, "Savior, like a shepherd, lead us," so Jesus commanded us to lead others to You. Thank You for this exciting process of growing in You. Thank You for the responsibility of discipling others that accompanies this growth.

So many infant Christians are wandering about without shepherds, and too many mature believers are not willing to pick up the cross of Jesus Christ. Forgive those of us who walk freely in intimate knowledge of You but are not sharing Your Word and shepherding others the way we are commanded.

Your Word tells us, "To whom much is given, much is required" (see Luke 12:48). I believe mature Christians are required by You to shepherd young Christians, for a time, according to Your instruction. Father, I often watch parent birds standing by their fledglings—protecting, feeding, and preening them until the baby birds can care for themselves. Help us as mature Christians to be this concerned for immature Christians. In Jesus' name. Amen.

Overworked Pastors

...Shepherd the flock of God which is among you, serving as overseers, not by compulsion but willingly, not for dishonest gain but eagerly... (I Peter 5:2, repeated verse)

Father, by Your Spirit, convict mature believers everywhere to stop relying on overworked leaders and pastors to do the work that You have called them to do. At the same time, Holy Spirit, equip pastors to admonish their congregations and guide their congregations lovingly in fruitful discipleship. Help pastors realize the importance of releasing congregations into the freedom of being led by Your Spirit.

Bring under conviction those pastors who are using control instead of letting Your Holy Spirit lead freely among Your people. Reveal to them that unless congregations are free to let Your Spirit work through everyone, Your Spirit will wait on the sidelines until freedom and liberty provides an atmosphere in which He can work.

The apostle Paul declared the whole counsel of Your Word so he would be "free of the blood of all innocent men" (Acts 20:26). Father, bring Christian leadership everywhere under that same conviction. May we be found doing our part to help Your Kingdom come on earth as it is in heaven. In Jesus' name. Amen.

Chapter Five
Leadership, Not Lordship

...nor as being lords over those entrusted to you, but being examples to the flock... (1 Peter 5:3)

Thank You, Father, for our glorious world and all the beauty we have to enjoy. You have entrusted Your creation to Your children, and it is an awesome responsibility! Even more awesome and challenging are the responsibilities that come with knowing You, growing in You, and helping others mature spiritually.

You remind leaders that we are not to act as lords over those You entrust to us, but we are to concentrate upon becoming examples that others might want to follow. Only You are our true Lord, so help us refrain from exalting ourselves, whether we are bosses, preachers, teachers, or strong leaders.

Satan uses this weakness of pride to his advantage. He uses our inclination to control others because of positions given us. Remind us that lives can be ruined with oppressive leadership, spiritual growth stifled, and young, growing Christians disappointed when leadership acts as "lords over those entrusted to them."

Help all church leadership to grow in humility and help us lead others to You, our true Lord, and not to ourselves. In Jesus' name. Amen.

Be Crowned!

> ...and when the Chief Shepherd appears, you will receive the crown of glory that does not fade away. (1 Peter 5:4)

Father, how mysterious this glory we learn about in Scripture and yet cannot fathom with our human minds! I immediately think of brightness, dazzling purity, and incomprehensible light. When I think of Jesus' coming back to earth in all of His glory, the full meaning and impact of it eludes me, but I rejoice for I know all creation groans as we await that blessed day.

Lord, You tell us that when the chief Shepherd appears, we will receive a crown of glory that does not fade away. Am I able to interpret these glorious words? I cannot, for the depth, the width, and the height of the meaning goes beyond my earthly ability to fully comprehend or explain. By faith, I rejoice in this good news!

Thank You, Lord, that I have this state of blessedness to look forward to as I am being changed into the likeness of Christ. As Jesus said in John 14:20, "At that day you will know that I am in my Father, and you in Me, and I in you."

Thank You that I am privileged to experience bits of earthly glory as I serve within Your will. Come, sweet Jesus, keep me faithful in daily, glorious service until You come. With Your help, I wait patiently for You. In Jesus' name. Amen.

Chapter Five

The Old Nature

Likewise you younger people, submit yourselves to your elders. Yes, all of you be submissive to one another, and be clothed with humility for "God resists the proud, but gives grace to the humble."
(1 Peter 5:5)

Father, as I walk through this life, there are times when I feel resistant to certain people, situations, or circumstances. In this resistance, I feel the strength of my old nature rearing its ugly head.

Perhaps a bad memory is triggered by someone or something, or there is a demand upon my already stressful life that creates more stress and sometimes anger. Forgive me my weaknesses. Truly "I Need Thee Every Hour!"

Thank You that You desire to clothe me in humility. This is a humility that buffers me against the stresses of life. Forgive me for tying Your hands by my lack of submission to You.

Continue to teach me. Help me live submitted to You, and subsequently to others, their cares, and their needs. Increase my desire to acknowledge my old nature and to resist pride. Mold and make me more into Your image. In His name. Amen.

The Spoiler

Likewise you younger people, submit yourselves to your elders. Yes, all of you be submissive to one another, and be clothed with humility for "God resists the proud, but gives grace to the humble."
(I Peter 5:5, repeated verse)

Lord, You tell us whether we are young in years or old, young in the Lord or somewhat mature in You, that we are to be submissive to one another and clothed in humility. What challenges You put before us when we attempt to walk in the Spirit! Your formula is perfect. Our response is, many times, imperfect.

Help me recognize pride at work in my life. Help me understand how Satan uses my pride to ruin my witness, spoil Your plans, and remove Your anointing that empowers my life. Surely Your gentle Holy Spirit withdraws when I succumb to wrong attitudes.

So help me to recognize the need for a submissive attitude. And then, heavenly Father, bless and empower me with more grace to live victoriously. In Jesus' name. Amen.

Chapter Five

Humbling Ourselves

Therefore humble yourselves under the mighty hand of God, that He may exalt you in due time...
(1 Peter 5:6)

Father, when I read the scriptures and think of what You have to say about humility, I realize that it is an important key to my relationship with You. And then, Father, I realize that pride is the direct opposite of humility. Oh, to be rid of pride and increase measurably in humility!

Pride seems to be a thorn in my side that continues to exercise itself intermittently. I know, Father, that if I deny that I have pride, I'm only fooling myself. I know that I am a new creature, born anew, washed in the blood, and filled with the Spirit. And yet my old nature sometimes rears its ugly head. It needs to be crucified. That is surely a daily growth process. I cannot do it on my own. Help me!

I humble myself through prayer today. I admit my faults. Please forgive me. I need Your help to walk under the influence of Your mighty hand that You might exalt me in Your time. Raise me up, fortify me, fill me, and gift me in proportion to the work You have for me this day.

According to the multitude of Your loving kindness, bless my life and efforts for building Your kingdom. In Jesus' name. Amen.

God Cares

...casting all your care upon Him, for He cares for you. (1 Peter 5:7)

O Father, there is so much pain in our world. Fear fills the hearts of many as our country seems to be in greater danger internally and externally than it has ever been before in our history. Terrorist activity is increasing all over our world, and the threat to peace looms like a dark cloud over us.

We face reality today, Lord Jesus, when we pray for our leadership in America and across our world. The forces of evil are real, and America needs Your wisdom and guidance more than ever before. Our Christian community is in need of maturity, so that each believer will become a hearer and a doer of Your Word.

Help us step out in service today by becoming a proclaimer of Your truth. The depth of Your love and caring must become real to the Christian community and to the world about us. Make us instruments who will declare Your Gospel, so we envelope others with Your love. Help us say and do the right things at the right time, according to the prompting of Your Holy Spirit.

Forgive us as a Church for setting ourselves aside as special or above those who don't attend worship services. Help us spread Your loving message beyond the organized Church to a needy world. Fill us with Your compassion and help us declare that love to the world, so they too will "Cast all their cares upon You, for You care for them." In the holy name of Jesus, I pray. Amen.

Chapter Five

Satan Is Real

Be sober, be vigilant; because your adversary the devil walks about like a roaring lion, seeking whom he may devour. (1 Peter 5:8)

Father, it seems that little by little You have awakened me to the many subtle and not so subtle activities of Satan on the earth. The closer I have grown to You, the more I have become aware of his activities. More importantly, You continue to open my eyes to the need for spiritual warfare and how believers must use the armor that You provide effectively (see Eph. 6:10-18).

When You warn us of Satan's intent, You tell us to "be sober." You're instructing us to realistically consider the ways he may try to accomplish his goals. I fear that many well-intentioned believers have taken wrong paths because they haven't been serious about the enemy and his dubious ways.

Satan steals our time, causes confusion, muddies our goals, spreads frustration, dulls Your voice, and causes us to be afraid of rejection for obedient behavior. Too often, we accept second-best when Satan is at work in our lives. Help us recognize his tactics and teach us how to use Your armor. In Jesus' name. Amen.

The Armor

Be sober, be vigilant; because your adversary the devil walks about like a roaring lion, seeking whom he may devour. (I Peter 5:8, repeated verse)

Father, cause me to deliberately put on Your whole armor and keep me vigilant as Satan sneaks around, trying to deceive. He deceives those who are trying to be faithful to You and also those who claim no particular allegiance or purpose for existence in this life.

Make me bold to deal with the devil when necessary and eager to put on Your armor daily. I am reminded to use the power of Jesus' name, the protection of His blood, and the public confession of my faith! (See Eph. 6:10-18.)

The closer we draw to You, dear Lord, the more clearly we will hear the roar of the devil as he walks about seeking whom he may devour. Satan is subtle. He never gives up on us. Help us to realize and protect ourselves against the many overtures he uses to erode our obedience to you—temptation, guilt, excuses, pride, discontent, the power of the misleading media, our subconscious mind, and defensive attitudes.

Keep us sober, keep us vigilant; keep us strong in faith, so that we are always poised to do battle, with confidence, when necessary. In the name of our true Counselor, Jesus Christ, I pray. Amen.

Chapter Five
Brotherhood Sufferings

Resist him, steadfast in the faith, knowing that the same sufferings are experienced by your brotherhood in the world. (1 Peter 5:9)

Precious Jesus, what joy the brotherhood of Christ brings to us! This deep knowledge that we share: who we are in You, the focus of our existence, the wonder of forgiveness, and the cleansing of Your precious blood that is so precious to us. Help us share with others the knowledge and daily experience of that overflowing fountain You have placed within us—joy unspeakable and full of glory.

Keep us faithful to gather with other Christians as we share our struggles and are strengthened in steadfast faith. These times of sharing, worship, and praise are focal points of renewing our strength in You.

We need each other in the brotherhood. We need the fellowship of sharing to maintain steadfastness in the faith. We need the purifying and undergirding love one to another that wondrously takes place when we come together.

Come, Holy Spirit, into our midst. Touch gently our sharing of love, commitment, and suffering. Thank You for working in the body of Christ all over the world. In Jesus' name. Amen.

Experience the Glory!

But may the God of all grace, who called us to His eternal glory by Christ Jesus, after you have suffered a while, perfect, establish, strengthen, and settle you. (1 Peter 5:10)

What beautiful understanding the apostle Peter has given us of suffering and how suffering is woven into our lives of discipleship! Peter tells us that suffering is a brotherhood experience in that it is an inevitable and natural part of belonging to the body of Christ. The many shades of suffering are surely intermingled with experiencing the earthly glory of serving You, O Lord.

Thank You, Lord, that suffering for Your sake perfects us, establishes us in You, strengthens us, and settles us into a life of obedience. To the extent that we are able to identify with You and the purpose for Your suffering, so shall we continue to be shaped and refined into Your image.

As darkness struggles with light in this present age, help us all endure adversity with eyes that are open to opportunities that will further Your cause. Demonstrate Your power through the body of Christ by helping us meet this adversity with Your enduring love, wisdom, and grace.

Continue to remind us, dear Lord, that believers have no license for retaliation or to commit attacks that result in defensiveness in those who do not have a relationship with You. We do not want our response to adversity to defeat Your purpose.

Continue to remind us that You will give sufficient grace for every challenge and that words spoken in Your perfect timetable always bring victory. Cause us to be patient in our suffering so we will experience shades of glory until that day when we shall experience eternal glory with You! In Jesus' name. Amen.

Chapter Five
Praise to the Lord!

To Him be the glory and the dominion forever and ever. Amen. (1 Peter 5:11)

Father, I come lifting holy hands as an act of praise today. Who can fathom Your glory? Perhaps one could better understand if "self" would step aside so that You, and only You would have complete dominion in our lives. It is our challenge to pray for that.

In the meantime, help us live as people of praise. In the midst of our praise, influence our lives the way You have planned from the beginning. Surely that would be glory for You and for us.

To You, precious Lord, we direct our praise. All honor, glory, power, dominion, and might be unto Your name forever and forever. Shine gloriously in our homes, our workplaces, and upon every footstep today, for we want You to govern our day.

Forever, O Lord, we pledge our allegiance for Your faithfulness endures to all generations. Indeed You established the earth, and how excellent is Your name in it! You have placed Your glory above the heavens.

When we consider the work of Your hands—all of creation that You have ordained—we marvel that You are mindful of us and call us Your children.

Holy, holy, holy are You, O Lord! Hear our prayer of praise, we pray, in Jesus' name. Amen.

Bonding

> By Silvanus, our faithful brother as I consider him, I have written to you briefly, exhorting and testifying that this is the true grace of God in which you stand. (1 Peter 5:12)

Thank You, Father, for the example of Silvanus (Silas), a true brother in Christ that You provided for Peter. How precious are the special people You allow us to bond with on this earth!

Father, we don't know all that Silas did that helped Paul fulfill Your purpose for his life; we rest assured that Silas lived through adversity with Paul and was there for him when the seas of life became rough. Paul called him a "faithful brother" in Christ. Help us be faithful to those with whom we share this life's journey.

Thank You for the richness of the epistle of First Peter and all that I have learned from studying, meditating and praying through these anointed scriptures. Father, the lessons have been deep, stretching, expanding, sometimes difficult, but always reassuring and faith-building.

You call this letter one that exhorts and one that testifies of Your true grace in which we stand. It has been that and so much more. Thank You for teaching us through prayer. Thank You for helping us relate to this letter from Peter as if he had penned it to the body of Christ today. Your anointed Word is alive and shall live forever to guide us into all righteousness. We yield our hearts today to that precious sanctifying power of the washing of the water of Your Word. In Jesus' name. Amen.

Chapter Five

Accountability

She who is in Babylon, elect together with you, greets you; and so does Mark my son. (1 Peter 5:13)

Thank You for Peter who spoke so powerfully and who continues to speak to those who will listen today. Peter is an example for us with the responsibility he assumed when he became a member of the body of Christ. Peter knew he not only represented himself and the cause of Christ, but he took upon himself the responsibility of representing the whole body of Christ. Teach us to do the same.

As the apostle Peter closes his letter, he lovingly refers to a relationship with the believers in Rome and credits Silas for assisting in the composition of First Peter.

Help us, too, become more accountable to the body of Christ that we represent. And Father, like Peter, help us give credit to those who assist us, for our good works are only possible through the helping hands and prayers of others that You are using in the body of Christ.

Father, we thank You that You teach and nurture us in every verse of Your Word when we stop long enough to listen to Your Holy Spirit. Slow us down, Lord, make us more contemplative, so that we may hear the still, small voice of Your Spirit who hovers over and around us daily. In Jesus' name. Amen.

Rich Tenderness

Greet one another with a kiss of love. Peace to you all who are in Christ Jesus. Amen. (1 Peter 5:14)

Greetings to You, wonderful Lord and Savior, Master of the universe and Creator of all mankind! I love You, Lord, and come into Your presence with a singing heart because of Your goodness, bountiful love, and grace.

The more I learn of You, the more profound Your ways seem to me. Truly the depth of the riches of Your wisdom and knowledge are unreachable. I thank You for growth in my relationship with You through praying the scriptures. How thankful I am for this experience as I have prayed the powerful epistle of First Peter back to You.

Father, You command us, through Peter, to always greet one another in love. This speaks an exhortation I need to hear often. Surely this love greeting to each other is one of vibrant reconciliation, acceptance, powerful love, and encouraging words. O Father, cleanse my heart anew as I speak to You in prayer.

Just as You always greet me with a kiss of love, assist me in greeting others with this same love that is joyful, accepting, and precious. How holy is this ministry of reconciliation! Thank You for Jesus' ultimate sacrifice on the cross and His words that resonate in my heart, "I in them and You in Me" (see Jo. 17:23).

Thank You for a multiplying peace as I pass on Your abundant love. Help me reach out today, and let all I do and say be of You, through You, and to You for Your glory! I pray continuously in the glorious name of Jesus Christ. Amen!

Topical Index

anointing	41,116
anxious, anxiety	65
armor	120
assurance	2
attitude	32,52,62-63
authorities, yielded to	46-47
balance	29,62
baptism	86
baptism in Holy Spirit	33
behavior	50,70-71
blessing others	4,69
blood	23,24,73,121
body of Christ	36,38-39,93,121
bonding	124
bondservant	49
born again	29
caregivers	2,43,70-71,92
catastrophes	36
Chief Cornerstone	37
chosen	1,2,35
cleansing	61,70-72
commands (oracles)	32,44,52,69,72,99
commitment	55-56,80-81,121
compassion	68-69
complete salvation	13
conduct	61
confidence	37,94,120
conscience	78,79
control	72,112-113
conviction	32
deceit	54
deliverance	13
devil	120
difficulties	36
discipling	111
disobedience	105
doing good	48,104,108
earnestness	33
edifying	93,111
elect	3

evil	32,45,51,65-66,69,70-71
expectation	91
faith	10,11,36,121
fair dealing	22
fear of the Lord	61
fellowship	121
flesh	44,46-47,59-60,82-83
forgiveness	10,32,95
foreordained	25
foundation	36
freedom	23,49,65-66,84,112
gentleness	64
gifts	34,97,98,99
glory	11,16,26,75-76,114,122-123
Godhead	86
good	51-53
grace	13,15,34,124
gratitude	4,96
growth, discipleship	33,102-103,111
guilt	29
habits	19
haven of rest	48
healing	41,57
heirs	67
holiness (holy)	20,21
holy priesthood	36,42
Holy Spirit	1-2,15-16,19,25,29,40-41,54,100,112
holy women	61,64
honor	50
hope	5,30
hospitality	97,108
humbling, humility	36,108,113,115-116
hypocrisy	32
impartiality	22
impatience	59-60
intercessor, intercession	87
infants	33
influence	62
inheritance	6
just, unjust	82-83
joy	12,26,29,40-41,92,129
judging, judgment	72,107,113

Lamb	24
leadership	33,50,109-110,113,118
liberty	49,102-103
light	42
living stone	35-37
long suffering	85
love	28,45,63,96
malice	32
marriage	67
mercy	5,43
minds	18
motivate, motivations	74,109-110
newborn	33
negative thoughts	32,70-71
obedience	16,19,80-81,119
opportunities	32
passion	1-2
patience	50,85
peace	30,97
people, special	42
persecution	75-76
perfect will	80-81,90
perfection	91
pilgrims, pilgrimage	1-2
power	5,7,9
praise	53,89,94,107,123
prayer	32,59-60,73,91,95
preach, preachers	31,84,111-112
precious	35,37-39
presence	31,88-89,97
pride	40-41,113,115,117
proclaimers	94
priests	36
prodigals	58
prophesy, prophecies	15-17
protection	75-76
quickening	48
quiet time	23
quietness	63-64
redeemed	24
redemption	23
rejection	35

rejoicing	9
repentance	44,72
rest	30,48
respect	50-51
responsibility	38-39,52,102-103,111,122
resurrection	26,86
retaliation	45,122
righteousness	73
role of women	65-67
salvation	13
sanctification, sanctify	49,77
Satan	116,120
saved	82-83
scales	33
seal	6
seeking	18,29,33,74
self-determination	40-41
self-sufficiency	40-41,105
sharing	121
sin, sinners	44,54,57,88,107
sober, sobriety	18
Solid Rock	36
song, the	63
spiritual house	36-37
spiritual sacrifices	36
strength	65-66
submission	46-47,51,55-56,59-60,64-66,116
suffer, suffering	52-53,75-76,80-81,88,101,104,108,122
tenseness	23
testing	10,36,120
thankfulness	3,36
threats	75-76
tolerance	69,102-103
tongue	20,70-71
traditions	23
transformation	90-91
trials	9,36,100
Trinity, the	86
unfair treatment	46-47
unrest	30,97
valleys of decision	58
victory	50

wholeness 57
will of God 80-81,90
witness 33,49,109-110,118
women, role of 64-67
Word (Scripture) 11,26-27,31-32,63,70-71,77,90,99
worship 31,61,94,96,104,107
yielded 46-47,59-60,80-81
yoked 74

About the Author

Mary Jane has been a caregiver for her husband, a stroke patient, for 12 years. As time allowed, she began meditating and praying through books of the Bible as an effective form of needed restoration; through this practice three manuscripts have evolved. Two have been published: *PRAYING THROUGH FIRST JOHN, Scale the Heights of God's Love!* and *PRAYING WITH PETER, Exciting Insights Into the Words of I Peter.*

Her experiences as mother, homemaker, grandmother, teacher, preacher, and caregiver have blessed her with a capacity to write with an appreciation for life. She and her husband reside in Mt. Carmel, Illinois.

Order copies by calling the author at 618-263-6060 or 618-263-8446. You may email her at the address below. Or order copies from any bookstore, Amazon.com, or Gazelle Press 800-367-8203.

To contact the author, please write:
Mary Jane Fischer
437 Park Rd., Mt. Carmel, IL 62863
Email: geomj@shawneelink.net